TITLES IN THIS SERIES
Edited and introduced by Mary-Alice Waters

The First and Second
Declarations of Havana

The First and Second Declarations of Havana

Manifestos of revolutionary struggle in the Americas adopted by the Cuban people

Pathfinder

NEW YORK   LONDON   TORONTO   SYDNEY

Edited by Mary-Alice Waters

Copyright © 2007 by Pathfinder Press

ISBN 978-0-87348-869-3
Library of Congress Control Number 2006940817
Manufactured in the United States of America

First edition, 1962
Second edition, 1994
Third edition, 2007
Second printing, 2007

FRONT COVER: Fidel Castro presenting the Second Declaration of
Havana to the Second National General Assembly of the Cuban
People in Havana's Plaza of the Revolution, February 4, 1962.
(*Bohemia*) The document was adopted by over one million Cubans,
and in the following days by hundreds of thousands more in
factories, fields, schools, and rallies across the island.
BACK COVER: Part of massive mobilization of Cubans at the February 4
Assembly. (Keystone/Getty Images)

COVER DESIGN: Eva Braiman

Pathfinder
www.pathfinderpress.com
E-mail: pathfinder@pathfinderpress.com

CONTENTS

PREFACE

This new expanded publication of the First and Second Declarations of Havana, issued simultaneously in Spanish and English, was born at the November 2006 Venezuela International Book Fair. It is the product of wide-ranging political discussions surrounding the presentation in Caracas of the two most recent issues of *Nueva Internacional*, a magazine of Marxist politics and theory, and of several books published by Pathfinder Press.

Today in Venezuela substantial numbers of workers, farmers, and student youth, as well as oppressed national minorities of many origins—African, indigenous, Chinese, Indian, Arab, and more—are being politicized by popular struggles that have been a driving force in Venezuelan politics the last decade. Struggles for land, for greater workers control over the safety, pace, and conditions of work, for access to education, health care, water, electricity, and housing. Struggles to retake control over the country's vast patrimony of natural resources. Defense of Venezuela's sovereign right to extend a hand of solidarity to oppressed and embattled peoples throughout the Americas and the world, including collaboration with the revolutionary government and people of Cuba. Resistance to economic sabotage by entrenched capitalist owners of industry, financial institutions, land, and means of communication, as well as their multiple attempts to oust the popularly elected government of Venezuela. Struggles marked by a growing popular awareness of the powerful imperialist interests inextricably intertwined with, and ultimately calling the shots for, Venezuela's capitalist class.

More than once since 1998, these conflicts have surged and ebbed and surged again over various issues and in different parts of the country, both exposing and being driven by deep social and political contradictions. Among the most committed of the popular forces, especially the youth, the thirst for a class perspective—a revolutionary socialist perspective—has grown, and along with it the thirst for a broader knowledge of the modern history of popular revolutionary movements. Why have some succeeded while others have failed?

This thirst was evident in the crowds thronging the stands and other events at the book fair. It marked the hours of nonstop political discussion and debate at the booth featuring books, pamphlets, and magazines distributed by Pathfinder Press, where the best-selling titles were the newest issues of *Nueva Internacional* featuring "Capitalism's Long Hot Winter Has Begun" and "Our Politics Start with the World" by Jack Barnes.

The questions debated were not insignificant.

Are the program and strategic course that resulted in the victory of workers and farmers in the Bolshevik-led 1917 October Revolution, as well as the debates that led to the formation in 1919 of a new revolutionary international—explained with such clarity by V.I. Lenin—still worth studying a century later? Or are the class forces shaping the world of the twenty-first century so fundamentally different that the Russian Revolution and the trajectory of the first five years of the Communist International are largely irrelevant? Are the political foundations of revolutionary activity today the same as those presented by Karl Marx and Frederick Engels?

Has the decreasing proportion of often landless rural toilers throughout Latin America relative to the growing size of the urban proletariat and layers of small traders and the jobless made the worker-farmer alliance an anachronism? Or does that alliance remain central to the very possibility of a successful revolutionary strategy for the working class?

Can capitalism be made to serve the interests of the toilers by establishing manufacturing cooperatives, comanagement ventures, and similar schemes? Or do the workings of capital, explained by Marx almost a century and a half ago, continue to dominate social relations so long as the working class has not taken power?

Are there progressive layers of the capitalist class in underdeveloped countries capable today of leading the militant toilers in struggle against imperialist domination? Or do these exploiters, no matter how rankled by the fetters of the imperialist masters, recoil from the revolutionary masses and act to suppress their struggles?

Has imperialism changed its spots? Or is a violent and bloody assault on the conquests of the working classes inevitable when the owners see a weakness that offers an opportunity to roll back inroads on their privileges and prerogatives?

Is socialism a set of ideas? Or is it—as Marx and Engels pointed out in the Communist Manifesto, and as has been confirmed in blood and sweat over a century and a half of popular struggles—the line of march of the working class toward power, a line of march "springing from an existing class struggle, from a historical movement going on under our very eyes"?

Nowhere are these kinds of questions that today confront men and women on the front lines of struggles in Latin America addressed with greater truthfulness and clarity than in the First and Second Declarations of Havana, presented by Cuban prime minister Fidel Castro and adopted by million-strong General Assemblies of the Cuban People on September 2, 1960, and February 4, 1962. That is why Pathfinder decided these declarations need to be broadly available today, presented in a way that helps make them and their interconnections more transparent and accessible to new generations of militants who did not live the tumultuous revolutionary events in the heat of which these documents were forged and signed on to by millions.

Included in this new Pathfinder book are more than a dozen pages of photos bringing those days alive and making them more understandable for readers today; a chronology situating in history the declarations themselves and the events they talk about, explaining references and inferences that those who heard or read these words nearly half a century ago understood without need of further comment; a glossary and notes identifying people and historical events otherwise unfamiliar to many readers today; and an index to aid those who will study and restudy these declarations with close attention.

While the Second Declaration of Havana has been more widely known since it was adopted some forty-five years ago, putting the First and Second Declarations together in the order they were presented is what makes it possible to place ourselves inside the historical turning points that linked them.

The first National General Assembly of the Cuban People was convoked on September 2, 1960, during the most intense period of mass mobilization the revolution had yet known. In the weeks before and after that outpouring, in response to the imperialists' increasing acts of armed terror and economic sabotage, hundreds of thousands of workers were taking control of more and more industrial enterprises in Cuba—factory after factory was "intervened," as Cuban workers termed it, and then nationalized by the revolutionary government.

In June 1960 three major imperialist-owned oil trusts in Cuba had announced their refusal to refine petroleum bought from the Soviet Union. Cuban workers responded by taking control of refineries owned by Texaco, Standard Oil, and Shell and refining the oil themselves. Within days U.S. president Dwight D. Eisenhower ordered punitive action, slashing by 95 percent the quota of sugar Washington had earlier agreed to import during the remaining months of 1960. Within seventy-two hours, the Soviet Union announced it would purchase all Cuban sugar the U.S. refused to buy.

Across the island, Cubans responded by defiantly proclaiming "*Sin cuota pero sin bota*"—without the U.S. market, but with the imperial boot no longer on our neck.

On August 6, as the capitalists' economic sabotage escalated, the revolutionary government adopted a decree expropriating the "assets and enterprises located on national territory . . . that are the property of U.S. legal entities." The following days and nights became known in Cuba as the Week of National Jubilation. Tens of thousands of Cubans celebrated by marching through the streets of Havana bearing coffins containing the symbolic remains of U.S. companies such as the United Fruit Company and International Telephone and Telegraph, tossing them into the sea.

By the end of October, Cuban workers and peasants, supported by their government, had expropriated virtually all imperialist-owned banks and industry, as well as the largest holdings of Cuba's capitalist class, including such icons as Bacardi rum. Together with the 1959 agrarian reform, which expropriated millions of acres of the largest landed estates and issued titles to some 100,000 landless peasants, property relations in city and countryside had been transformed, definitively establishing the character of the revolution as socialist—the first in the hemisphere— and making clear to all that state power now served the historic interests of working people.

Participating alongside the Cuban people in the events of this historic turning point were many of the nearly one thousand young people from across Latin America, as well as the United States, Canada, the Soviet Union, China, and elsewhere, who had traveled to Cuba to take part in the First Latin American Youth Congress that opened July 26, 1960, in the Sierra Maestra mountains. Among those who that summer were convinced of the necessity, and the possibility, of emulating the revolutionary road traveled by the Cuban people were a good many of the future leaders of revolutionary struggles throughout the Americas. This included young leaders of the Socialist Workers Party and Young Socialist Alliance in the United States.

It was Che Guevara, in his welcoming speech to the youth congress delegates on July 28, who explained to them—and to the world—that "if this revolution is Marxist—and listen well that I say 'Marxist'—it is because it discovered, by its own methods, the road pointed out by Marx."

As this tumultuous transformation was unfolding, the foreign ministers of the member countries of the Organization of American States met in San José, Costa Rica, at the end of August. Under the guiding hand of Washington, they adopted a resolution that, while never mentioning Cuba by name even once, condemned "energetically the intervention . . . by an extra-continental power in the affairs of the American republics"; rejected the "attempt of the Sino-Soviet powers to make use of the political, economic, or social situation of any American state," as a course endangering "the peace and security of the hemisphere"; declared that the "inter-American system is incompatible with any form of totalitarianism" [one could only wish!]; and proclaimed that "all member states . . . are under obligation to submit to the discipline of the inter-American system."

This was the "Declaration of San José" answered September 2 by the "Declaration of Havana." Extending "the hand of friendship to the people of the United States—including Black people subjected to lynching, persecuted intellectuals, and workers forced to accept the leadership of gangsters," the National General Assembly of the Cuban People searingly replied that imperialist domination of Latin America and the policies of the U.S. government were the reason "the peace and security of the hemisphere and the world" were endangered.

The assembly affirmed "that the unsolicited offer of the Soviet Union to aid Cuba if our country is attacked by imperialist military forces cannot be considered an act of intervention, but rather a clear act of solidarity." And it proclaimed openly and publicly "before the Americas and the world that it accepts with gratitude the help of rockets from the Soviet Union should our territory be invaded by military forces of the United States."

It rejected with indignation the self-serving, U.S.-instigated OAS document alleging that the Cuban Revolution was the product of Soviet or Chinese intervention in the Americas as opposed to "the just response of Cuba to crimes and injuries perpetrated by imperialism in Latin America." It announced that the Cuban government would immediately establish diplomatic relations with the People's Republic of China and break all ties with Taiwan.

It condemned "the exploitation of man by man, and the exploitation of the underdeveloped countries by imperialist finance capital" as the real obstacle to democracy and freedom in the Americas and pledged that the Cuban people would not fail their brothers and sisters of Latin America who "take up the arms of liberty."

～

"Politics begin where millions of men and women are; where there are not thousands, but millions. That is where serious politics begin," Lenin reminded delegates to the 1918 congress of the Russian Communist Party (Bolshevik) a few months after the triumph of the October Revolution. That is the power that speaks through the First and Second Declarations of Havana, the power evident in the photos included here of those immense concentrations of confident, joyous, and determined toilers in the midst of deciding their own future.

The year and a half between the First and Second Declarations was marked above all by the "serious politics" of millions.

• Cuban prime minister Fidel Castro's September 1960 presentation of "The Case of Cuba" before the General Assembly of the United Nations, which he ended by citing the closing portions of the First Declaration of Havana summarizing what the Cuban Revolution stands for;

• the mobilizations across the island accompanying the revolutionary government's Urban Reform Law nationalizing housing, slashing rents to 10 percent of a family's income, and thus putting an end, in the words of the Second Declaration of Havana, to "the abusive system that turned housing into a means of exploiting people";

• Washington's decision to break diplomatic relations with Havana;

• the mobilization of 100,000 young people to the furthest reaches of the countryside and working-class barrios in the massive, successful campaign that wiped out illiteracy in Cuba in less than a year (establishing the model for the hundreds of thousands of Cuban volunteer teachers and medical personnel who in coming decades would put their training to use among those oppressed by imperialism the world over);

• the U.S.-organized and -financed invasion of Cuba at the Bay of Pigs in April 1961, which ended less than seventy-two hours later in ignominious defeat with the surrender of the invading mercenaries;

• the beginning of the first "Freedom Rides" across the U.S. South to challenge Jim Crow segregation in interstate public transportation;

• Che Guevara's denunciation at Punta del Este, Uruguay, in August 1961 of the fraud of the U.S. government's newly launched Latin American "Alliance for Progress";

• Cuba's first internationalist aid to Africa, sending arms and ammunition to Algeria's National Liberation Front (FLN) fighting French colonial rule and providing treatment to wounded combatants as well as housing and education to orphans of the war;

• the imposition of a total trade embargo against Cuba by the U.S. government on February 3, 1962.

What was the Cuban people's response to the announcement that foreign ministers of the Organization of American States would meet in Punta del Este in late January 1962 to consider collective measures to counter "the threat to the peace and political independence of the American states" arising from intervention by "extra-continental powers"?

"Now that they're preparing the stage to carry out the puppets' farce," Fidel announced to a mass rally on January 2 celebrating the third anniversary of the victory over the tyranny, "let's mobilize!"

> When is the foreign ministers meeting? The twenty-second? Very well then, on the 22nd we are also going to mobilize here at the Plaza of the Revolution! [*Prolonged applause*] On the 22nd we're going to convene the Second General Assembly of the Cuban People! [*Applause*] And we are going to proclaim the Second Declaration of Havana! [*Applause*] The entire people. It will not just be the people of Havana, it will come from other provinces, anyone who is able to come, and it will be the most gigantic event of the revolution, of the people [*Applause*] to present to the world the Second Declaration of Havana, and to show the imperialists our readiness to fight, and to show the puppets what a revolutionary people is, what a free people is, what a heroic people is! [*Applause*]

On February 4 over a million Cubans answered that call to arms, effectively repudiating the resolutions adopted four days earlier by what they referred to as the "Yankee ministry of colonies." The OAS foreign ministers meeting in Punta del Este unanimously condemned a supposed "subversive offensive of communist governments" whose aim "is the destruction of democratic institutions and the establishment of totalitarian dictatorships at the service of extra-continental powers"; declared that "the present government of Cuba, which has officially identified itself as a Marxist-Leninist government, is incompatible with the principles and objectives of the inter-American system"; expelled Cuba from the OAS; established an Inter-American Defense Council watchdog committee against "subversion," with executive powers; and urged that appropriate steps be taken by member states for their individual and collective self-defense.

As the National General Assembly of the Cuban People clarified: "For the Yankee imperialists, 'subversion' means the struggle of hungry people for bread, the struggle of peasants for land, the struggle of the peoples against imperialist exploitation. A watchdog committee with executive powers within the Inter-American Defense Council means a continental repressive force against the peoples, a force under the command of the Pentagon. 'Collective measures' means the landing of Yankee marines in any country of the Americas."

"What is it that is hidden behind the Yankees' hatred of the Cuban revolution," the assembly asked? What is it that unites

> for the same aggressive ends the richest and most powerful imperialist power in the contemporary world and the oligarchies of an entire continent . . . against a small country of only 7 million inhabitants, economically underdeveloped, without financial or military means that could threaten the security or economy of any other country? . . .
>
> What unifies them and incites them is fear. . . . Not fear of the Cuban Revolution, but fear of the Latin American revolution. . . . Fear that the plundered people of the continent will seize the arms from their oppressors and, like Cuba, declare themselves free peoples of the Americas.

This perspective of the revolutionary struggle to take political power from the capitalists and defend it arms in hand is what lies at the center of the Second Declaration of Havana. The affirmation of the courage and political organization necessary to accomplish that task. The vista opened by a rising wave of revolutionary struggles throughout the Americas, and the example of the Cuban

201

workers and farmers proving, "Yes, it can be done."

The impact the Second Declaration of Havana had at the time is hard to appreciate without recalling that the necessity, and possibility, of the plundered peoples of the continent emulating the road to power of the Cuban workers and farmers was precisely what was denied—and feared— by the large majority of parties throughout Latin America that fraudulently wore the label worker, or communist, or socialist. "The duty of every revolutionist is to make the revolution," not "sit in the doorways of their houses waiting for the corpse of imperialism to pass by"—not to wait for supposedly unripe objective conditions to ripen, as many parties claimed to be doing. That ringing declaration was a fresh wind sweeping through the Americas.

Most important, the declaration effectively explained to the vanguard of workers, farmers, and revolutionary-minded youth increasingly engaged in struggles throughout the Americas, including the United States, why the possibilities of success were in their hands and none others.

• It explained why the national bourgeoisie is incapable of leading a struggle against imperialist domination "even when its interests are in contradiction to those of Yankee imperialism . . . for the national bourgeoisie is paralyzed by fear of social revolution and frightened by the cry of the exploited masses."

• It explained why no revolution could succeed unless the working class was capable of leading the struggle in the countryside as well, forging and continuously working to maintain a powerful alliance in struggle with the peasantry, with the oppressed indigenous peoples of the Americas, with the Blacks, the Chinese, and the other superexploited sections of the population. Over and over, it pointed to the importance of the unfolding mass struggles by Blacks to bring down the system of Jim Crow segregation in the United States.

• It explained how unity in action of the toilers against imperialism and its agents, without which no revolutionary victory is possible, could be achieved only if sectarianism, dogmatism, and the deliberate fostering of division as opposed to common struggle could be eradicated.

• It explained the "bloody drama" Washington and its puppets were preparing for Latin America—one that soon became all too real—as the great masses of the continent began to rise in struggle, and the fatal illusion of believing in the possibility under such conditions of "wresting power by legal means, means that do not and will not exist, from the hands of ruling classes that are entrenched in all the state positions," a power they "will defend by blood and fire and with the might of their police and armies."

And it pointed to the revolutionary victory at Playa Girón—Washington's first military defeat in the Americas—as the example that the Cuban people gave to the world "that revolution is possible."

~

These were lessons the Cuban people themselves were writing in blood with their own struggles in the months that linked the First and Second Declarations of Havana. They remain as true today as they were nearly fifty years ago, as true as they have been since 1848.

It is in that spirit that this new presentation of the First and Second Declarations of Havana is being published.

And it is to those who will use it in that manner that it is dedicated.

Mary-Alice Waters
January 2007

The
First Declaration
of Havana

En la Asamblea más grande del mundo,

EL PUEBLO DECIDIO:

REVOLUCION

ORGANO DEL MOVIMIENTO 26 DE JULIO

2ª EDICION — Año III ● La Habana, Sábado, 3 de Sept. de 1960 — 5 Centavos ● DIRECTOR: CARLOS FRANQUI ● No. 537

LA ASAMBLEA GENERAL NACIONAL DEL PUEBLO DE CUBA PROCLAMA ANTE AMERICA

- Aprobar la "Declaración de La Habana"
- Rechazar la declaración de Costa Rica
- Aceptar la ayuda de la URSS y de China
- Romper el tratado militar con EE. UU.
- Establecer relaciones con China Popular
- Emplazar a los gobiernos latinoamericanos a que convoquen a sus pueblos
- *Proclamar los derechos del hombre latinoamericano*

VEA EN LA PAGINA 3: TEXTO DEL DISCURSO DE FIDEL

Front page of *Revolución*, daily newspaper of the July 26 Movement, September 3, 1960, following approval of the First Declaration of Havana by the National General Assembly of the Cuban People.

It reads: "In the world's largest assembly THE PEOPLE DECIDED: To approve the 'Declaration of Havana'; to reject the declaration of Costa Rica; to accept aid from the USSR and China; to break the military treaty with the U.S.; to establish relations with People's China; to challenge the governments of Latin America to convene their peoples as we are doing; to proclaim the rights of man in Latin America."

The First Declaration of Havana

Adopted by the National General Assembly
of the Cuban People

September 2, 1960

At the foot of the monument in memory of José Martí, the people of Cuba, Free Territory of the Americas, acting with inalienable powers flowing from an effective exercise of sovereignty through direct, public, and universal suffrage, have constituted themselves the National General Assembly.

In its own name, and expressing the sentiments of the people of Our America, the National General Assembly of the Cuban People:

1. Condemns in its entirety the so-called Declaration of San José, Costa Rica, a document dictated by U.S. imperialism that violates the sovereignty and dignity of other peoples of the continent and the right of each nation to self-determination.[1]

---

1. The Organization of American States (OAS) held its Seventh Consultative Meeting of Foreign Ministers of the American Republics in San José, Costa Rica, August 22–29, 1960. There the OAS approved the

2. The National General Assembly of the Cuban People strongly condemns U.S. imperialism for its gross and criminal intervention carried out for more than a century against all the peoples of Latin America, who more than once have seen the soil of Mexico, Nicaragua, Haiti, Santo Domingo, and Cuba invaded; who have lost to the greedy Yankee imperialists such wide and rich lands as Texas, such vital strategic zones as the Panama Canal, and even, as in the case of Puerto Rico, entire countries converted into territories of occupation; who have suffered insults by the marines toward our wives and daughters and toward the most cherished memorials of the history of our lands, among them the figure of José Martí.[2]

That intervention, built on military superiority, on unfair treaties, and on the shameful submission of traitorous governments, has for more than a hundred years transformed Our America—the America that Bolívar, Hidalgo, Juárez, San Martín, O'Higgins, Sucre, Tiradentes, and Martí sought to free—into a zone of exploitation, a backyard of the Yankee financial and political empire, and a reserve supply of votes in international organizations, where we of the Latin American countries have always been regarded as beasts of burden to a "rough and brutal North that scorns us."[3]

Declaration of San José. This document asserted that all member states were "under obligation to submit to the discipline of the inter-American system." The Cuban delegation submitted a counterresolution and, after it was defeated, walked out of the meeting.

2. On March 11, 1949, several members of the U.S. Navy were photographed climbing atop the statue of José Martí in Havana's Central Park, which they urinated on. As word of the desecration spread, demonstrations and protests erupted. Among the leaders of the protests was Fidel Castro.

3. From José Martí's 1895 letter to Manuel Mercado. See pages 37–38.

The National General Assembly of the People declares that Latin American governments, by accepting this unremitting and historically indisputable intervention, betray the ideals of independence, destroy the sovereignty of their peoples, and obstruct true solidarity among our countries. For these reasons this Assembly, in the name of the Cuban people, repudiates this domination with a voice embodying the hopes and determination of the peoples of Latin America and in the same spirit of liberation that motivated the immortal fathers of the Americas.

The submission of traitorous governments has made Our America a backyard of the Yankee empire

3. The National General Assembly of the People rejects as well the attempt to perpetuate the Monroe Doctrine, until now utilized, as José Martí foresaw, "to extend the domination in America" of greedy imperialists and to inject more easily "the poison of loans, of canals, and railroads," a poison also denounced in a timely way by José Martí.

Therefore, in opposition to that hypocritical Pan-Americanism that is nothing more than the domination of our peoples' interests by Yankee monopolies and the prostration of governments before Washington, the Assembly of the Cuban People proclaims the liberating Latin Americanism of José Martí and Benito Juárez. Furthermore, while extending the hand of friendship to the people of the United States—including Black people subjected to lynching, persecuted intellectuals, and workers forced to accept the leadership of gangsters—the Assembly reaffirms its will to march "with the whole world and not just a part of it."

4. The National General Assembly of the People declares that the unsolicited offer of the Soviet Union to aid Cuba if our country is attacked by imperialist military forces cannot be considered an act of intervention, but rather a clear act of solidarity. Such aid, offered to Cuba in the face of an imminent attack by the Pentagon, honors the government of the Soviet Union as much as cowardly and criminal aggressions against Cuba dishonor the government of the United States. Therefore, the General Assembly of the People declares before the Americas and the world that it accepts with gratitude the help of rockets from the Soviet Union should our territory be invaded by military forces of the United States.

5. The National General Assembly of the Cuban People categorically denies the [Declaration of San José's] charge that there has been any attempt by the Soviet Union and the People's Republic of China "to make use of the economic, political, and social situation" in Cuba "in order to break continental unity and to endanger hemispheric unity." From the first to the last volley, from the first to the last of the twenty thousand martyrs who fell in the struggle to overthrow the tyranny and take revolutionary power, from the first to the last revolutionary law, from the first to the last act of the revolution, the people of Cuba have moved of their own free will. Therefore, no grounds exist for blaming either the Soviet Union or the People's Republic of China for the existence of a revolution that is the just response of Cuba to crimes and injuries perpetrated by imperialism in Latin America.

To the contrary, the National General Assembly of the Cuban People believes that the peace and security of the hemisphere and the world are endangered by the policy advanced by the government of the United States—and imposed upon the governments of Latin America—a policy of hostility and isolation toward the Soviet Union and the People's Republic of China, of warlike and aggressive acts, and of systematically excluding the People's Republic of China from the United Nations, despite the fact that it represents nearly all the 600 million inhabitants of China.[4]

Therefore, the National General Assembly of the Cuban People ratifies its policy of friendship with all the peoples of the world and reaffirms its intention to establish diplomatic relations with all the socialist countries. The Assembly, exercising its free and sovereign will, informs the People's Republic of China of its decision to establish diplomatic relations with it, thereby rescinding ties with the puppet regime maintained in Formosa by the Yankee Seventh Fleet.

6. The National General Assembly of the Cuban People—confident that it is expressing the general opinion of the people of Latin America—affirms that democracy is incompatible with financial oligarchy; with discrimination against Blacks and Ku Klux Klan outrages; with the persecution that drove scientists such as Oppenheimer from their posts, deprived the world for years of the marvelous voice of Paul Robeson, held prisoner in his own country, and sent the Rosenbergs to their death over the protests of a shocked world, including appeals by many governments and of Pope Pius XII.

The National General Assembly of the Cuban People expresses Cuba's conviction that democracy does not consist solely of elections that are almost always managed by wealthy landowners and professional politicians in order to

---

4. At the time, China's UN seat was occupied by the government of Taiwan, also sometimes referred to as Formosa. In 1971 the People's Republic of China assumed the seat.

produce fictitious results, but rather in the right of citizens to determine their own destiny, as this General Assembly of the Cuban People is now doing. Furthermore, democracy will be realized in Latin America only when people are really free to make choices, when the poor are not reduced—by hunger, social discrimination, illiteracy, and the judicial system—to frightful powerlessness.

Therefore, the National General Assembly of the Cuban People:

Condemns the backward, inhuman landed-estate system of agricultural production, a source of misery and poverty for the rural population. It condemns starvation wages and the grossly unjust exploitation of human labor by illegitimate and privileged interests. It condemns illiteracy, the lack of teachers, schools, doctors, hospitals, and care for the elderly that prevails in Latin America. It condemns the discrimination against Blacks and Indians. It condemns the inequality and exploitation of women. It condemns the military and political oligarchies that keep our peoples in utter misery and hinder the development toward democracy and the full exercise of their sovereignty. It condemns the handing over of our countries' natural resources to the foreign monopolies as a policy of concessions that surrenders and betrays the interests of the peoples. It condemns the governments that ignore the sentiments of their people in order to obey Washington's dictates. It condemns the systematic deception of the people by the news media in the interests of the oligarchies and the imperialist oppressor. It condemns the monopoly of the news media by Yankee agencies, instruments of the U.S. trusts and agents of Washington. It condemns repressive laws that prevent workers, peasants, students, and intellectuals—the great majority of each country—from organizing to fight for their social demands and patriotic aspirations. It condemns the imperialist monopolies and companies that constantly plunder our wealth, exploit our workers and peasants, bleed our economies and keep them in backwardness, and force Latin America, in matters of policy, to submit to their designs and interests.

In short, the National General Assembly of the Cuban People condemns the exploitation of man by man, and the exploitation of the underdeveloped countries by imperialist finance capital.

We condemn the exploitation of man by man, and of the underdeveloped countries by finance capital

Therefore, the National General Assembly of the Cuban People proclaims before the Americas:

The right of peasants to the land; the right of workers to the fruit of their labor; the right of children to education; the right of the sick to medical and hospital care; the right of the young to a job; the right of students to free education that is both practical and scientific; the right of Blacks and Indians to "full human dignity"; the right of women to civil, social, and political equality; the right of the elderly to a secure old age; the right of intellectuals, artists, and scientists to use their work to fight for a better world; the right of states to nationalize the imperialist monopolies, thereby recovering their national wealth and resources; the right of countries to engage freely in trade with all the peoples of the world; the right of nations to their full sovereignty; the right of the peoples to turn garrisons into schools, and to arm their workers, peasants, students, intellectuals, Blacks,

Indians, women, young people, old people, and all the oppressed and exploited, so they themselves may defend their rights and their destiny.

7. The National General Assembly of the Cuban People affirms:

The duty of workers, peasants, students, intellectuals, Blacks, Indians, youth, women, the elderly, to fight for their economic, political, and social rights; the duty of oppressed and exploited nations to fight for their liberation; the duty of every people to solidarize with all the oppressed, exploited, colonized, and aggrieved peoples wherever they are regardless of distance or geographical separation. All peoples of the world are brothers!

8. The National General Assembly of the Cuban People affirms its faith that Latin America, united and victorious, will soon be free of the bonds that now make its economies rich spoils for U.S. imperialism; that keep its true voice from being heard at conferences where tamed foreign ministers form a sordid chorus to the tune of the despotic masters. The Assembly ratifies, therefore, its decision to work for this common Latin American destiny, which will allow our countries to build a true solidarity, founded on the free decision of each and the common goals of all. In this fight for a liberated Latin America, and against the obedient voice of those who hold office as usurpers, there now arises with invincible power the genuine voice of the people, a voice that breaks through from the depths of coal and tin mines, from factories, and sugar mills, from feudal lands where rotos, cholos, gauchos, jíbaros,[5] the heirs of Zapata and Sandino, take up the arms of liberty; a voice that finds expression in its poets and novelists,

---

5. Rural workers from Chile, Peru, Argentina, and Puerto Rico, respectively.

in its students, in its women and children, in its old and sleepless.

To this voice of our brothers, the National General Assembly of the Cuban People responds:

Presente! Cuba will not fail.

As a historic pledge before Latin America and the world, Cuba is here today to proclaim its unbreakable decision: *Patria o muerte!*

9. The National General Assembly of the Cuban People resolves that this declaration shall be known as the "Declaration of Havana."

HAVANA, CUBA
Free Territory of the Americas
September 2, 1960

Front page of Cuban daily *Revolución*, February 5, 1962, following approval of Second Declaration of Havana by National General Assembly of the Cuban People. In photo at top are Prime Minister Fidel Castro and President Osvaldo Dorticós.

The headlines read: "This great humanity has said: 'Enough!' More than a million in the Assembly. We will resist in all fields. The entire people approve the Second Declaration of Havana. This struggle will be waged by the masses, by the people."

Fidel Castro presents Second Declaration of Havana.

The Second Declaration of Havana

Adopted by the National General Assembly
of the Cuban People

February 4, 1962

From the people of Cuba to the peoples of the Americas
and the world:

On May 18, 1895, on the eve of his death from a Spanish bullet through the heart, José Martí, apostle of our independence, wrote in an unfinished letter to his friend Manuel Mercado:

> Now I am able to write. . . . I am in danger each day now of giving my life for my country and for my duty . . . of preventing the United States, as Cuba obtains her independence, from extending its control over the Antilles and, consequently, falling with that much more force upon our American lands. Whatever I have done up til now, and whatever I shall do, has been with that aim. . . .
>
> The nations most vitally concerned in preventing Cuba from becoming, through its annexation by the imperialists, the road to the annexation of the countries of Our America by the rough and brutal North that scorns them—something

that must be prevented, and which we are preventing with our blood—are being held back by commitments of a public and lesser order from openly supporting and joining in this sacrifice, which we are making for their direct benefit.

I have lived inside the monster and know its entrails; and my sling is the sling of David.

In 1895 Martí had already pointed to the danger looming over the Americas and called imperialism by its name: imperialism. He pointed out to the people of Latin America that they, more than anyone, had a stake in seeing to it that Cuba did not succumb to Yankee greed and scorn of the peoples of Latin America. And with his own blood, shed for Cuba and Latin America, he signed the words that long after his death, in homage to his memory, the people of Cuba affirm today at the opening of this declaration.

Sixty-seven years have passed. Puerto Rico was converted into a colony and remains a colony saturated with military bases. Cuba also fell into the clutches of imperialism, and imperialist troops occupied our territory. The Platt Amendment was imposed on Cuba's first constitution, as a humiliating clause that sanctioned the odious right of foreign intervention.[1] Our wealth passed into their hands, our history was falsified, our government and our politics were molded entirely in the interests of the overseers. The nation was subjected to sixty years of political, economic, and cultural suffocation.

But Cuba rose up. Cuba redeemed itself from the bas-

---

1. Cuba's final war for independence from Spain, fought from 1895 to 1898, was immediately followed by a U.S. military occupation of the country. For the Platt Amendment and similar historical references, see the glossary.

tard tutelage. Cuba broke the chains that tied its fortunes to those of the imperial oppressor, reclaimed its wealth, reaffirmed its culture, and unfurled its sovereign banner of Free Territory and People of the Americas.

Now the United States will never again be able to use Cuba's strength against the Americas. Conversely, the United States, dominating the majority of the other Latin American states, today attempts to use the strength of the Americas against Cuba.

What is the history of Latin America if not the history of imperialist exploitation?

What is the history of Cuba if not the history of Latin America? What is the history of Latin America if not the history of Asia, Africa, and the Pacific? And what is the history of all these peoples if not the history of imperialism's pitiless and cruel exploitation throughout the world?

At the end of the last century and the beginning of the present one, a handful of economically developed nations had finished partitioning the world among themselves, subjecting to their economic and political domination two-thirds of humanity forced to work for the ruling classes of the economically advanced capitalist countries.

The historical circumstances that permitted a high level of industrial development to some European countries and to the United States of America placed them in a position to subject the rest of the world to their domination and exploitation.

What were the compelling motives behind the expansion of the industrial powers? Were their reasons moral and "civilizing," as they claim? No, the reasons were economic.

From the discovery of America, a discovery that launched the European conquerors across the seas to occupy and exploit the lands and inhabitants of other continents, the fundamental motive for their conduct has been the desire for riches. The discovery of America itself came about as they searched for shorter routes to the Orient, whose goods fetched a high price in Europe.

A new social class, the merchants and the producers of manufactured articles for commerce, arose from the womb of the feudal society of lords and serfs during the waning Middle Ages.

The thirst for gold was the spring that moved the efforts of that new class. The lust for profit has been the incentive that drove the conduct of that class throughout history. With the growth of manufacturing and commerce, its social influence also grew. The new productive forces developing in the womb of feudal society clashed more and more with feudalism's relations of servitude—its laws, its institutions, its philosophy, its morality, its art, and its political ideology.

The intellectual representatives of the bourgeois class proclaimed new philosophical and political ideas, new concepts of law and of the state, which—because they responded to the new necessities of social life—gradually entered into the consciousness of the exploited masses. These were at the time still revolutionary ideas, ideas opposed to the outmoded notions of feudal society. The peasants, the artisans, the workers in manufacture, led by the bourgeoisie, overthrew the feudal order, its philosophy, its ideas, its institutions, its laws, and the privileges of the ruling class, that is, of the hereditary nobility.

At that time the bourgeoisie considered revolution necessary and just. It did not believe that the feudal order could and should be eternal—as it now considers its capitalist social order to be.

It encouraged the peasants to free themselves from feudal servitude; it encouraged the artisans against the medieval guilds; and it demanded the right to political power. The absolute monarchs, the nobility, and the clerical hierarchy stubbornly defended their class privileges, proclaiming the divine right of kings and the immutability of the social order. To be liberal, to proclaim the ideas of Voltaire, Diderot, or Jean-Jacques Rousseau—spokesmen for bourgeois philosophy—constituted, in the eyes of the ruling classes of that time, as serious a crime as it is today, in the eyes of the bourgeoisie, to be a socialist and to proclaim the ideas of Marx, Engels, and Lenin.

The bourgeoisie took political power and established upon the ruins of feudal society its capitalist mode of production; and on the basis of this mode of production it built its state institutions, its laws, its ideas. Those institutions sanctified above all the essence of its class rule: private property.

The new society based on the private ownership of the means of production and free competition was thus divided into two basic classes: one the owner of the means of production, ever more modern and efficient; the other, deprived of all wealth, possessing only its labor power, a labor power of necessity sold on the market as any other commodity, simply in order to survive.

With the feudal bonds broken, the productive forces developed extraordinarily. Great factories arose in which larger and larger numbers of workers were assembled.

The most modern and technically efficient factories continually displaced from the market their less efficient competitors. The cost of industrial equipment continually rose. It became necessary to accumulate more and more capital. A greater portion of production passed into a smaller number of hands. Thus arose the large capitalist enterprises and later, according to the degree and character of the association, the great industrial combines through cartels, syndicates, trusts, and consortiums, controlled by the owners of the major portion of the stock, that is to say, by the most powerful heads of industry. Free competition, characteristic of capitalism in its first phase, gave way to monopolies, which entered into agreements among themselves and controlled the markets.

"Capital comes into the world dripping from every pore with blood and dirt," wrote Karl Marx.

Where did the colossal resources come from that permitted a handful of monopolists to accumulate billions of dollars? From the exploitation of human labor. Millions of workers, forced to toil for bare subsistence wages, produced with their labors the gigantic capital of the monopolies. The workers amassed the fortunes of the ever richer, ever more powerful privileged classes. Through the banks these classes were able to make use not only of their own money but that of all society. Thus came about the fusion of the banks with large-scale industry, and finance capital was born. What should they do with the huge surplus of capital that was accumulating in ever greater quantities? Invade the world with it. Ever in pursuit of profit, they began seizing the natural resources of all the economically weak countries and exploiting the human labor of the inhabitants, imposing wages even more wretched than what these classes are compelled to pay workers in their own developed countries. Thus began the territorial and economic division of the world. By 1914 eight or ten imperialist countries had subjugated territories beyond their own borders covering more than 83.7 million square kilometers, with a population of 970 million inhabitants. They had simply divided up the world.

But as the world, limited in size, was divided to the last corner of the earth, a clash ensued among the different monopolist nations. Struggles arose for new divisions, originating in the disproportionate distribution of industrial and economic power the various monopolistic nations had attained in their uneven development. Imperialist wars broke out that would cost humanity fifty million dead, tens of millions of invalids, and the destruction of incalculable material and cultural wealth. Even before this had happened, Karl Marx wrote that "capital comes into the world dripping from head to foot, from every pore, with blood and dirt."

The capitalist system of production, once it had given all it was capable of, became an abysmal obstacle to the progress of humanity. But the bourgeoisie from its origins carried within itself its antithesis. In its womb gigantic productive instruments were developed. With time, however, a new and vigorous social force expanded: the proletariat, destined to change the old and outmoded social system of capitalism to a higher socioeconomic form in accordance with the historic possibilities of human society, converting into social property those gigantic means of production that the people—and no one else but the people—had created and amassed by their labor. At such a stage of development of the productive forces, it became completely anachronistic and outmoded to have a regime that stood for private ownership and with it the economic subordination of millions and millions of human beings to the dictates of a small minority of society.

The interests of humanity cried out for a halt to the anarchy of production, the waste, economic crises, and rapacious wars that are integral to the capitalist system. The growing needs of the human race and the possibility of satisfying those needs, demanded the planned development of the economy and rational utilization of its means of production and natural resources.

It was inevitable that imperialism and colonialism would fall into a profound and unsolvable crisis. The general world crisis was announced by the outbreak of World War I, with the revolution of the workers and peasants that overthrew the tsarist empire of Russia and founded, amid the most difficult conditions of capitalist encirclement and aggression, the world's first socialist state, opening a new era in the history of humanity. From that time until today, the crisis and decomposition of the imperialist system has steadily worsened.

World War II, unleashed by the imperialist powers— into which were dragged the Soviet Union and other criminally invaded peoples of Asia and Europe, forcing them into a bloody struggle of liberation—culminated in the defeat of fascism, formation of the world camp of socialism, and the struggle of the colonial and dependent peoples for their sovereignty. Between 1945 and 1957 more than 1.2 billion human beings conquered their political independence in Asia and Africa. The blood shed by the peoples was not in vain.

The movement of the dependent and colonial peoples is a phenomenon universal in character that agitates the world and places its mark on the final crisis of imperialism.

Cuba and Latin America are part of the world. Our

problems are part of the problems engendered by the overall crisis of imperialism and the struggle of the subjugated peoples, the clash between the world being born and the world that is dying. The odious and brutal campaign unleashed against our nation expresses the desperate as well as futile effort that the imperialists are making to prevent the liberation of the peoples.

Our problems are part of the clash between the world being born and the world that is dying

Cuba affronts the imperialists in a special way. What is it that is hidden behind the Yankees' hatred of the Cuban Revolution? What is it that rationally explains the conspiracy—uniting for the same aggressive ends the richest and most powerful imperialist power in the contemporary world and the oligarchies of an entire continent, which together are supposed to represent a population of 350 million human beings—against a small country of only 7 million inhabitants, economically underdeveloped, without financial or military means that could threaten the security or economy of any other country?

What unifies them and incites them is fear. What explains it is fear. Not fear of the Cuban Revolution, but fear of the Latin American revolution. Not fear of the workers, peasants, intellectuals, students, and progressive layers of the middle strata who by revolutionary means have taken power in Cuba, but fear that the workers, peasants, students, intellectuals, and progressive sectors of the middle strata will take power by revolutionary means in the oppressed and hungry countries exploited by the Yankee monopolies and reactionary oligarchies of the Americas; fear that the plundered people of the continent will seize the arms from their oppressors and, like Cuba, declare themselves free peoples of the Americas.

By crushing the Cuban Revolution they hope to dispel the fear that torments them, the specter of revolution that threatens them. By eliminating the Cuban Revolution, they hope to eliminate the revolutionary spirit of the people. They imagine in their delirium that Cuba is an exporter of revolutions. In their sleepless merchants' and money lenders' minds lives the idea that revolutions can be bought, sold, rented, loaned, exported and imported like a piece of merchandise. Ignorant of the objective laws that govern the development of human societies, they believe that their monopolistic, capitalistic, and semifeudal regimes are eternal. Educated in their own reactionary ideology—a mixture of superstition, ignorance, subjectivism, pragmatism, and other mental aberrations—they have an image of the world and of the march of history conforming to their interests as exploiting classes.

They imagine that revolutions are born or die in the brains of individuals or are caused by divine laws, and moreover that the gods are on their side. They have always thought that way—from the devout pagan patricians of Roman slave society who hurled the early Christians to the lions at the circus, through the Inquisitors of the Middle Ages who, as guardians of feudalism and absolute monarchy, burned at the stake the first representatives of liberal thought of the nascent bourgeoisie, up to today's bishops who anathematize proletarian revolutions in defense of bourgeois and monopolist regimes.

All reactionary classes in all historical epochs, when the antagonism between exploiters and exploited reaches its highest peak, foretelling the arrival of a new social system, have turned to the worst weapons of repression and calumny against their adversaries. The early Christians were sent to their martyrdom accused of burning Rome and of sacrificing children on their altars. Philosophers like Giordano Bruno, reformers like Hus, and thousands of others who did not conform to the feudal order were accused of heresy and taken by the Inquisitors to be burned at the stake.

Today persecution rages over the proletarian fighters, a crime whose way is paved by the worst calumnies in the monopolist and bourgeois press. Always, in each historic epoch, the ruling classes have committed murder. They do so invoking the "defense of society, order, country"—their "society" of the privileged minority against the exploited majority; their class "order," maintained by blood and fire against the dispossessed; the "country," whose fruits only they enjoy, depriving the rest of the people—all this to repress the revolutionaries who aspire to a new society, a just order, a country truly for all.

But the development of history, the ascending march of humanity, cannot, and will not, be halted. The forces that impel the people, who are the real makers of history, are determined by the material conditions of their existence and by the aspirations for higher goals of well-being and liberty that emerge when man's progress in the fields of science, technology, and culture make this possible. These forces are superior to the will and the terror unleashed by the ruling oligarchies.

The subjective conditions of each country, the conscious factor—organization and leadership—can, according to its greater or lesser degree of development, accelerate or retard the revolution. But sooner or later, in each historic epoch, when the objective conditions mature, consciousness grows, organization develops, leadership emerges, and revolutions take place.

Whether this takes place peacefully or in painful birth does not depend on the revolutionists; it depends on the reactionary forces of the old society, who resist the birth of the new society engendered by the contradictions carried in the womb of the old. Revolution historically is like the doctor who assists at the birth of a new life. It does not use the tools of force without reason, but will use them without hesitation whenever necessary to help the birth, a birth that brings to the enslaved and exploited masses the hope of a better life.

Whether revolutions take place peacefully or in painful birth does not depend on the revolutionists

In many countries of Latin America, revolution is today inevitable. That fact is not determined by anyone's will. It is determined by the horrifying conditions of exploitation in which Latin Americans live, the development of the revolutionary consciousness of the masses, the global crisis of imperialism, and the worldwide movement of struggle of the subjugated peoples.

The restlessness felt today is an unmistakable symptom of rebellion. The very depths of a continent are being shaken, a continent that has witnessed four centuries of slave, semislave, and feudal exploitation beginning with its original inhabitants and slaves brought from Africa, up to the nuclei of nationalities that emerged later: white, Black, mulatto, mestizo, and Indian, who are today made brothers by scorn, humiliation, and the Yankee yoke, and are brothers in their hope for a better tomorrow.

The peoples of Latin America freed themselves from Spanish colonialism at the beginning of the last century, but they did not free themselves from exploitation. The feudal landowners assumed the authority of the Spanish rulers, the Indians continued in painful servitude, Latin Americans in one form or another remained slaves, and the tiniest hopes of the people gave way under the power of the oligarchies and yoke of foreign capital. This has been the truth of Latin America—in one hue or another, in one variation or another. Today Latin America lies beneath an imperialism fiercer, crueler, and more powerful than the Spanish colonial empire.

In face of the objective reality and historically inexorable Latin American revolution, what is the attitude of Yankee imperialism? To prepare to wage a colonial war against the peoples of Latin America; to create an apparatus of force, the political pretexts, and the pseudolegal instruments subscribed to by the reactionary oligarchies to suppress the struggle of the Latin American peoples in blood and fire.

The intervention of the government of the United States in the internal politics of the countries of Latin America has become increasingly open and unbridled.

The Inter-American Defense Council, for example, has been and remains the nest where the most reactionary and pro-Yankee officers of the Latin American armies are trained for later use in carrying out coups in the service of the monopolies.

The U.S. military missions in each nation of Latin America constitute a permanent apparatus of espionage directly tied to the Central Intelligence Agency, inculcating in those Latin American officers the most reactionary sentiments and trying to convert these armies into instruments of their own political and economic interests.

In the Panama Canal Zone, the U.S. high command has organized special courses to train Latin American officers to fight against revolutionary guerrillas, with the aim of repressing the armed action of the peasant masses against the feudal exploitation to which they are subjected.

In the United States itself, the Central Intelligence Agency has organized special schools to train Latin American agents in the most sophisticated methods of assassination; and within the Yankee military services the physical elimination of anti-imperialist leaders is established policy.

The Yankee embassies in the different Latin American countries are notorious for organizing, instructing, and equipping fascist bands to spread terror and to attack labor, student, and intellectuals' organizations. These bands—into which they recruit the sons of the oligarchies, the lumpen, and individuals of the lowest moral character—have already perpetrated numerous acts of aggression against the mass movements.

Nothing reveals more clearly and unequivocally the intentions of imperialism than its recent conduct in the events in Santo Domingo.[2] With no justification, without even making use of diplomatic relations with that republic, the United States, after stationing warships off the Dominican capital, declared with its usual arrogance that if Balaguer's

---

2. In November 1961, amid growing rebellion in the Dominican Republic against the U.S.-backed government of Joaquín Balaguer, Washington sent warships off the Dominican coast. The rebellion was triggered by the return to Santo Domingo of two brothers of former dictator Rafael Leónidas Trujillo, assassinated six months earlier. Several years later, in April 1965, over twenty thousand U.S. troops invaded the Dominican Republic to crush a popular uprising led by supporters of Juan Bosch, whose government had been overturned in a military coup two years earlier.

government sought military aid, the U.S. would land troops in Santo Domingo against the insurgence of the Dominican people. That Balaguer's power was absolutely spurious, that each sovereign country of Latin America should have the right to resolve its internal problems without foreign intervention, that there exist international norms and world opinion, even that there exists an OAS, counted as nothing in the considerations of the United States.

What did count were its designs to hold back the Dominican revolution, the reinstitution of the odious policy of landing marines, with no more basis or prerequisite for establishing this new, pirate concept of law than the simple request of a tyrannical, illegitimate, crisis-ridden ruler. The significance of this should not escape the Latin American peoples. In Latin America there are more than enough of the kind of rulers who are ready to use Yankee troops against their own people when they find themselves in crisis.

U.S. imperialism's stated policy of sending troops to fight the revolutionary movement of any country in Latin America, that is, to kill workers, students, peasants, Latin American men and women, has no other objective than the maintenance of its monopolistic interests and the privileges of the traitorous oligarchies that support it.

It can now be seen clearly that the military pacts signed by the government of the United States with Latin American governments—often secret pacts and always behind the back of the people—invoking hypothetical foreign dangers that no one has ever seen, had the sole and exclusive aim of impeding struggles by the people. They were pacts against the people, against the sole danger imperiling Yankee interests—the internal danger of the liberation movement in each country. It was not without reason that the people asked themselves: Why so many military pacts? Why the shipment of arms that, even though technically outmoded for modern war, are still effective for smashing strikes, repressing popular demonstrations, staining the land with blood? Why the military missions, the Rio de Janeiro Pact,[3] and the thousand and one international conferences?

Since the end of World War II, the nations of Latin America have been impoverished more and more; their exports have less and less value; their imports cost more; per capita income falls; the frightful rate of infant mortality does not decrease; the number of illiterates is higher; the people lack jobs, land, adequate housing, schools, hospitals, means of communication, and means of life. On the other hand, U.S. investments now exceed $10 billion. Latin America, moreover, is a provider of cheap raw materials and a buyer of expensive finished goods. Like the first Spanish conquerors, who bartered mirrors and trinkets for gold and silver—that is how the United States trades with Latin America. To guard that torrent of riches, to gain ever more control of Latin America's resources and exploit its suffering peoples— that is what is hidden behind the military pacts, the military missions, and Washington's diplomatic intrigues.

This policy of gradual strangulation of the sovereignty of the Latin American nations and of a free hand for imperialism to intervene in their internal affairs culminated in the recent meeting of foreign ministers at Punta del Este.[4] Yankee imperialism gathered the ministers together

---

3. The Inter-American Treaty of Reciprocal Assistance was signed on September 2, 1947, in Rio de Janeiro by twenty-one governments, including the United States. It declared that aggression against any treaty member state would be considered an attack on all of them.

4. Punta del Este, Uruguay, was the site of a January 22–31, 1962, meeting of foreign ministers of Latin America and the United States, sponsored by the Organization of American States (OAS). The meeting

to wrest from them—through political pressure and un-precedented economic blackmail in collusion with a group of the most discredited rulers of this continent—the re-nunciation of our peoples' national sovereignty and the consecration of the Yankees' odious right to intervene in the internal affairs of Latin America. To wrest from them the total submission of the people to the will of the United States of North America, against which all our great men, from Bolívar to Sandino, have fought. Neither the govern-ment of the United States, nor the representatives of the ex-ploiting oligarchies, nor the big reactionary press in the pay of the monopolies and feudal lords tried to disguise their aims. They openly demanded agreements that constituted formal suppression of the right of self-determination of our peoples, abolishing it with a stroke of the pen in the most infamous conspiracy in this continent's memory.

Cuba speaks for the exploited of Latin America; the United States, for the exploiters

Behind closed doors, in repugnant secret meetings where the Yankee minister of colonies devoted entire days to beat-ing down the resistance and scruples of various ministers, bringing the Yankee treasury's millions into play in an undisguised buying and selling of votes, a handful of rep-resentatives of the oligarchies of countries barely adding up altogether to a third of the continent's population imposed

---

expelled Cuba from the OAS and called for Latin American support to military action against Cuba. Cuba's delegation was headed by President Osvaldo Dorticós, who condemned the imperialist moves.

agreements serving up to the Yankee master on a silver platter the head of a principle that has cost the blood of all our countries since the wars of independence.

The Pyrrhic character of such pathetic and fraudulent accomplishments of imperialism, its moral failure, the broken unanimity and universal scandal do not diminish the grave danger that agreements imposed at such a price have brought so close to the peoples of Latin America. At that immoral conclave, Cuba's thundering voice was raised without weakness or fear, indicting before all the peoples of America and the world the monstrous attack and defending—with a manliness and dignity that will go down in the annals of history—not only the rights of Cuba but the forsaken rights of all our sister nations of the American continent. The words of Cuba found no echo in that housebroken majority, but neither could they find a refutation; only impotent silence met Cuba's devastating arguments, the clarity and courage of its words. But Cuba was not speaking to the ministers, Cuba was speaking to the people and history. There its words will be echoed and find a response.

At Punta del Este a great ideological battle unfolded between the Cuban Revolution and Yankee imperialism. Who did each side represent, for whom did each one speak? Cuba represented the people; the United States represented the monopolies. Cuba spoke for the exploited masses of Latin America; the United States for the exploiting, oligarchic, and imperialist interests. Cuba for sovereignty; the United States for intervention. Cuba for the nationalization of foreign enterprises; the United States for even greater investments by foreign capital. Cuba for culture; the United States for ignorance. Cuba for agrarian reform; the United States for great landed estates. Cuba for the industrialization of the Americas; the United States for underdevelopment. Cuba for creative work; the United States for sabotage and counterrevolutionary terror practiced by its agents—destruction of sugarcane fields and factories, bombing by their pirate planes of the work of a peaceful people. Cuba for the murdered literacy workers; the United States for the murderers.[5] Cuba for bread; the United States for hunger. Cuba for equality; the United States for privilege and discrimination. Cuba for the truth; the United States for lies. Cuba for liberation; the United States for oppression. Cuba for the bright future of humanity; the United States for the past without hope. Cuba for the heroes who fell at Girón to save the country from foreign domination;[6] the United States for the mercenaries and traitors who serve the foreigner against their own country. Cuba for peace among peoples; the United States for aggression and war. Cuba for socialism; the United States for capitalism.

The agreements obtained by the United States, using methods so shameful that the entire world condemns them, do not diminish but increase the morality and justice of

---

5. During the early years of the revolution, Washington organized, financed, and supplied counterrevolutionary bands that committed acts of sabotage and terror in the countryside and cities across Cuba.

Among the victims were nine volunteer teachers and their students who were part of the successful 1961 campaign led by the revolutionary government to wipe out illiteracy in a single year. By the end of the effort one million Cubans had learned to read and write, largely through the mobilization of 100,000 young people who went to the countryside and isolated working-class districts, where they lived with peasants and workers.

6. On April 17, 1961, 1,500 Cuban-born mercenaries invaded Cuba at the Bay of Pigs on the southern coast. The action, organized by Washington, aimed to establish a "provisional government" that would immediately appeal for direct U.S. intervention. But the invaders, never able to secure a foothold, were defeated in less than seventy-two hours by the militia and the revolutionary armed forces and police. On April 19 the last invaders surrendered at Playa Girón (Girón Beach), which is the name Cubans use to designate the battle.

Cuba's stand, a stand that exposes how the oligarchies sell out and betray the national interest and shows the people the road to liberation. It reveals the rottenness of the exploiting classes of Latin America for whom their representatives spoke at Punta del Este. The OAS was revealed for what it really is—a Yankee ministry of colonies, a military alliance, an apparatus of repression against the liberation movement of the Latin American peoples.

Organization of American States: the Yankee ministry of colonies

Cuba has lived three years of revolution with incessant harassment, incessant Yankee intervention in our internal affairs. Pirate airplanes coming from the United States, dropping incendiary matériel, have burned tens of millions of pounds of sugarcane. Acts of international sabotage perpetrated by Yankee agents, such as blowing up the ship *La Coubre*, have cost dozens of Cuban lives.[7] Thousands of U.S. weapons have been parachuted into our territory by the U.S. military services to promote subversion. Hundreds of tons of explosive materials and infernal devices have been secretly landed on our coast from U.S. launches to promote sabotage and terrorism. A Cuban worker was tortured on the Guantánamo naval base and deprived of his life with no due process beforehand nor any explanation afterward.[8] In

7. On March 4, 1960, the French ship *La Coubre*, bringing Belgian munitions purchased by Cuba, blew up in Havana harbor, killing 101 people.

8. On October 19, 1961, Rubén López Sabariego, a Cuban freight-truck driver, was arrested by U.S. troops at the U.S. naval base at Guantánamo on the southeast coast of Cuba. Days later his body, showing signs of

order to ruin our economy, our sugar quota was abruptly cut[9] and an embargo proclaimed on parts and raw materials for factories and U.S.-manufactured machinery. Cuban ports and installations have been subject to surprise attacks by armed ships and bombers from bases prepared by the United States. Mercenary troops, organized and trained in Central American countries by that same government, have invaded our territory, escorted by ships of the Yankee fleet and with air support from foreign bases, causing much loss of life and material wealth. Counter-revolutionary Cubans are being trained in the U.S. army, and new plans of aggression are being made against Cuba. All this has been going on for three years without let-up, before the eyes of the whole continent . . . and the OAS knows nothing about it?

The ministers meet in Punta del Este and do not even admonish either the U.S. government or the governments that are material accomplices to these aggressions. They

---

torture, was found by other Cuban workers on territory belonging to the base.

The U.S. naval station was established during the U.S. occupation at the beginning of the twentieth century. Under the terms of the agreement imposed on Cuba, Washington's tenure over the base has no time limit and can be abrogated or modified only by mutual agreement. Over the protests of the Cuban people and government, the Guantánamo base remains there to this day.

9. The sugar quota was the amount of Cuban sugar Washington allowed to be sold in the U.S. market. In July 1960 the U.S. government ordered a cut in Cuba's sugar quota by 700,000 tons—slashing imports by 95 percent for the remainder of the year. Cuban sugar imports were later eliminated altogether. In October 1960 Washington declared a partial embargo on trade with Cuba. A total embargo was imposed by President Kennedy on February 3, 1962, the day before the Second Declaration of Havana was presented. This brutal embargo has been maintained and tightened, with bipartisan support, ever since.

expel Cuba, the Latin American victim, the aggrieved nation.

The United States has military pacts with nations of all continents, military blocs with whatever fascist, militarist, and reactionary government there is anywhere in the world: NATO, SEATO, and CENTO, to which we now must add the OAS. The United States intervenes in Laos, in Vietnam, in Korea, in Formosa, in Berlin. It openly sends ships to Santo Domingo to impose its law, its will, and announces its aim of using its NATO allies to block commerce with Cuba . . . and the OAS knows nothing about it? The ministers meet and expel Cuba, which has no military pacts with any country. Thus the government organizing subversion throughout the world and forging military alliances on four continents forces the expulsion of Cuba, accusing it, no less, of subversion and ties beyond the continent.

Cuba is the Latin American nation that has made landowners of more than 100,000 small farmers[10] and ensured year-round employment on state farms and cooperatives to all agricultural workers. It has transformed garrisons into schools; given seventy thousand scholarships to university, secondary, and technical students; created classrooms for the entire population of children; totally wiped out illiteracy. It has quadrupled medical services; nationalized foreign interests; suppressed the abusive system that turned housing into a means of exploiting people. It has virtually eliminated unemployment; suppressed discrimi-

---

10. The agrarian reform law of May 17, 1959, set a limit of 30 caballerías (approximately 1,000 acres) on individual landholdings. Implementation of the law resulted in confiscation of the vast estates in Cuba, many of them owned by U.S. companies, which passed into the hands of the new government. The law also granted sharecroppers, tenant farmers, and squatters deeds to the land they tilled.

nation on account of race or sex; rid itself of gambling, vice, and administrative corruption; armed the people. It has made the enjoyment of human rights a living reality by freeing men and women from exploitation, lack of culture, and social inequality. It has liberated itself from all foreign tutelage, acquired full sovereignty, and established the foundations to develop its economy in order, no longer, to be a country producing only one crop, sugar, and exporting only raw materials.

And yet it is Cuba that is expelled from the Organization of American States by governments that have not realized for their people any one of these achievements. How will they be able to justify their conduct before the peoples of the Americas and the world? How will they be able to deny that, according to their political conceptions, it is the policy of land, bread, work, health, liberty, equality, and culture; of accelerated development of the economy, of national dignity, of full self-determination and sovereignty that is incompatible with the principles of the hemisphere?[11]

The people think very differently. The people think the only thing incompatible with the destiny of Latin America is misery, feudal exploitation, illiteracy, starvation wages, unemployment; the policy of repression against the masses of workers, peasants, and students; discrimination against women, Blacks, Indians, mestizos; oppression by the oligarchies, the plundering of their countries' wealth by the Yankee monopolists; the moral suffocation of their intellectuals and artists; the ruin of the small producers by foreign competition; economic underdevelopment; peoples without roads, without hospitals, without housing, without

---

11. A refrain throughout the Punta del Este resolutions was that Cuba's course was "incompatible with the principles and objectives of the inter-American System."

schools, without industries; submission to imperialism; renunciation of national sovereignty and betrayal of the country.

How can the imperialists make their conduct toward and condemnation of Cuba understood? What words and what arguments will they use to speak to those whom, all the while exploiting them, they have ignored for so long?

Those who study the problems of Latin America are accustomed to asking: Which country has addressed the situation of the destitute, the poor, the Indians, the Blacks, and the helpless infants—this immense number of infants, 30 million in 1950, which will be 50 million in eight more years. Yes, which country?

32 million Indians form the backbone of the American continent

Thirty-two million Indians form the backbone—like the Andes Mountains—of the entire American continent. For those who considered the Indian more a thing than a person, this mass of humanity does not count, did not count, and, they believed, never would count. Since they were considered a brute labor force, they were to be used like a yoke of oxen or a tractor.

How could anyone believe in any benefit from imperialism, in any Alliance for Progress[12] with imperialism—

---

12. The Alliance for Progress was a U.S.-sponsored program established in 1961 as a response to the Cuban Revolution and its example. It allocated $20 billion in loans to Latin American governments over a ten-year period in exchange for their compliance in lining up against Cuba.

whatever it promised—when under its saintly protection the natives of the south of the continent, like those of Patagonia, still experience its massacres and its persecutions, still live under strips of canvas as did their ancestors at the time the discoverers came almost five hundred years ago? Those great races that populated northern Argentina, Paraguay, and Bolivia, such as the Guaraní who were savagely decimated, are hunted like animals and buried in the depths of the jungle. The extinction of that reservoir of indigenous stock—which could have served as a basis for a great Latin American civilization—is being accelerated. Across the Paraguayan swamps and desolate Bolivian highlands, deeper into itself, Latin America has driven these primitive, despondent races, their minds destroyed by alcohol and narcotics to which they resort in order at least to survive in the subhuman conditions (subhuman not just in diet) in which they live.

A chain of hands stretches out, still almost fruitlessly— as they have been stretching out fruitlessly for centuries. Over the Andean peaks and slopes, along great rivers and in the shadowy forests, this chain of hands stretches to unite their miseries with those of others who are slowly perishing—Brazilian tribes and those of the north of the continent and the coasts, to the hundred thousand Motilón Indians of Venezuela, who live in the most incredible backward and savage conditions, confined to the Amazon jungle or the Perijá mountain ranges, then to the isolated Vapicharnas, who await their end, now almost definitively lost to the human race, in the hot regions of the Guianas. Yes, all these 32 million Indians, who extend from the U.S. border to the edges of the Southern Hemisphere, and the 45 million mestizos, who for the most part differ little from the Indians; all these natives, this formidable reservoir of labor, whose rights have been trampled on—yes, what can imperialism offer them? How can these people, ignored so long, be made to believe any benefit can come from such bloodstained hands?

Entire tribes that still live unclothed; others that are labeled cannibals; others whose members die like flies upon their first contact with the conquering civilization; others that are banished, thrown off their lands, shunted off to the forests, mountains, or most distant reaches of the plains, where not even the smallest particle of culture, light, bread, or anything else penetrates.

In what "alliance"—other than one for their own more rapid extermination—are these native races to believe, these races who have been flogged for centuries, shot so their lands could be taken, beaten to death by the thousands for not working fast enough to the benefit of imperialist exploitation?

And the Blacks? What "alliance" can the system of lynching and brutal exclusion of Blacks in the United States offer to the 15 million Blacks and 14 million mulattos of Latin America, who know with horror and rage that their brothers to the north cannot ride in the same vehicles as their white compatriots, nor attend the same schools, nor even die in the same hospitals?

How are these spurned and rejected racial groups to believe in this imperialism, in its benefits or in any "alliance" with it (other than an alliance to lynch and exploit them as slaves)? Those masses who have not been permitted to even modestly enjoy cultural, social, or professional benefits, who—even when they are in the majority, or number in the millions—are mistreated by the imperialists in Ku Klux Klan garb, are confined to the most unsanitary neighborhoods, in the least comfortable tenements built expressly for them, are shoved into the most menial occupations, the hardest labor, and the least lucrative employment, who don't attend universities, top academies, or private schools.

What Alliance for Progress can serve as encouragement to those 107 million men and women of Our America, the backbone of labor in the cities and fields, whose dark skin—Black, mestizo, mulatto, Indian—inspires derision in the new colonialists? How are they—who in bitter helplessness have seen in Panama one wage scale for Yankees and another for Panamanians, who are regarded as an inferior race—going to put any trust in the supposed Alliance?

How are Blacks in the U.S. to believe in imperialism's benefits?

What can the workers hope for, with their starvation wages, the hardest jobs, the most miserable conditions, malnutrition, illness, and all the evils fostered by misery?

What words can be said, what benefits can the imperialists offer to the copper, tin, iron, and coal miners who cough up their lungs for the profits of merciless foreign masters? Or to the fathers and sons who work in the timberlands, the rubber, *mate*, and fruit plantations, the coffee and sugar mills? Or to the peons on the pampas and plains who with their health and lives amass the fortunes of the exploiters?

What can those vast masses expect, those who everywhere produce the wealth, who create the value, who aid in bringing forth a new world? What can they expect from imperialism, that greedy mouth, that greedy hand, with no vista beyond that of misery, the most absolute destitution and, at the end, a cold and unrecorded death?

What can this class expect, a class that has changed the course of history in other parts of the world, that has revolutionized the world, that is the vanguard of all the humble and exploited? What can it expect from imperialism, its most irreconcilable enemy?

What can imperialism offer the teachers, professors, professionals, intellectuals, poets, and artists? What benefits, what hopes for a better and more equitable life, what purpose, what inducement, what desire to excel, to go beyond the first simple steps? What can it offer those who devotedly care for the generations of children and young people on whom imperialism will later gorge itself? What can it offer these people who in most countries live on degrading wages, who almost everywhere suffer restrictions on their right to political and social expression, whose economic prospects do not exceed the stark limits of their insecure resources and income, who are buried in a dismal life with no future, one that ends on a pension not even meeting half the cost of living? What "benefits" or "alliances" can imperialism offer them, save those that redound completely to its own advantage?

If imperialism gives assistance to the professions, arts, and publications, it is always well understood that their output must reflect imperialism's interests, its aims, and its "nothingness."

But what of the novels that attempt to reflect the real world of imperialism's rapacious deeds? The poems aspiring to translate protests against imperialism's enslavement, its interference in life, in thought, in the very bodies of nations and peoples? The militant arts that try to express the forms and content of imperialism's aggression; that try to capture the constant pressure on everyone who lives, and give encouragement to all that is revolutionary? Anything that teaches—anything full of light and conscience, of clar-

> *"In this fight for a liberated Latin America, the Cuban people respond: 'Presente!' Cuba will not fail."*

Top: Fidel Castro, wearing traditional straw hat of Cuban peasants, reads the First Declaration of Havana, September 2, 1960. **Bottom**: Part of crowd of one million at National General Assembly of the Cuban People. Sign at left says, "Cuba, beacon of freedoms." Sign at center warns would-be invaders of Cuba: "Those who come stay."

"The Cuban people have made human rights a living reality by freeing men and women from exploitation, lack of culture, and social inequality."

Working people in Cuba resisted counterrevolutionary attacks by Washington and by U.S. and Cuban capitalists and landlords. As workers "intervened" workplaces to combat economic disruption, the revolutionary government nationalized U.S. and large Cuban enterprises between August and October 1960.

Facing page, top: Telephone worker chisels name off formerly U.S.-owned Cuban Telephone Company, August 1960. **Bottom**: Celebration of success of year-long literacy campaign, Havana, December 1961, by tens of thousands of young volunteers who by the end of the effort had taught almost one million workers and peasants to read and write. Nine Cubans—literacy volunteers and peasants who were studying—were murdered by U.S.-backed counterrevolutionaries in 1961. **This page, top**: Camagüey province, 1942, Cuban peasants being evicted from farms. **Bottom**: After revolution, under May 1959 agrarian reform, 100,000 Cuban farmers received title to land they tilled.

NUEZ / REVOLUCIÓN

"At Punta del Este, Cuba was not speaking to the OAS ministers, Cuba was speaking to the people and history, where its words will find an echo and a response."

Facing page, top: Ernesto Che Guevara denounces imperialist exploitation of Latin America at Organization of American States meeting, Punta del Este, Uruguay, August 1961. Six months later, also in Punta del Este, OAS expelled Cuba at Washington's behest. **Bottom**: Cuban newspapers ridiculed OAS as U.S. puppet and cover for mercenaries who invaded Cuba at Playa Girón. **This page**: Popular mobilizations took place across Americas in early 1960s condemning U.S. attacks: **(top)** Fair Play for Cuba Committee protest outside UN building in New York, November 1960; **(center)** Caracas, Venezuela, July 26, 1960; **(bottom)** La Paz, Bolivia, April 1961.

> *"Where the road is closed to the people, it is not right to beguile them with the illusion of wresting power from entrenched ruling classes by legal means, a power these classes will defend by blood and fire."*

This page, top: At December 1962 Miami rally, U.S. president John F. Kennedy welcomes home Cuban mercenaries captured at Playa Girón. From left: counterrevolutionary Manuel Artime; José Miró Cardona, first prime minister of Cuba in 1959 replaced by Fidel Castro in February; Kennedy and First Lady Jacqueline Bouvier Kennedy. **Bottom**: Dictator Fulgencio Batista receives solid gold telephone from U.S.-owned Cuban Telephone Company, in gratitude for approving large-scale rate increases in March 1957. **Facing page top and center**: Cuba's revolutionary armed forces, militias, and police crush April 1961 invasion by 1,500 U.S.-backed mercenaries at Playa Girón on Bay of Pigs. **Bottom**: Women in Santo Domingo confront U.S. troops following Washington's April 1965 invasion of Dominican Republic.

"This anonymous mass of the Americas has begun to write its own history."

Top: Tin miners, holding dynamite, protest killing of student demonstrators in Oruro, Bolivia, October 1964. **Center**: Mass peasant unions in La Convención Valley, Peru, demand land, early 1960s. Banner proclaims, "Land or death. We will win." **Bottom**: Panamanians call for sovereignty over U.S.-controlled canal, November 1959.

Top: Demonstrators met with police firehoses during 1963 Battle of Birmingham, Alabama, a battleground in U.S. civil rights movement watched worldwide. **Bottom**: "Betancourt, the people brought you back from exile…Now you're their assassin," says sign carried by demonstrator in Venezuela, protesting December 1960 police killings at University of Caracas. Following the popular overthrow of a military dictatorship in 1958, Rómulo Betancourt returned to Venezuela to become president of a pro-U.S. regime that used increasing brutality against workers, peasants, and youth fighting for economic and social progress.

"It is not for revolutionists to sit in their doorways
waiting for the corpse of imperialism to pass by."

One million Cubans poured into the Plaza of the Revolution, February 4, 1962, to demonstrate support for the Second Declaration of Havana and their determination to carry it out.

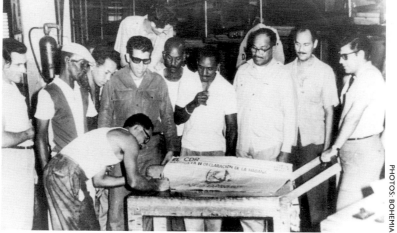

"The epic struggle before us will be carried forward by our peoples, mistreated and scorned by the imperialists, invisible to them until today, in whom Yankee monopoly capitalism now sees its gravediggers."

Masses of Cuban workers and farmers signed the Second Declaration of Havana, adding their names to the list of gravediggers.

ity and beauty—that tries to guide men and peoples to better destinies, to the highest summits of life and justice? All these meet imperialism's severest censure. They run into obstacles, condemnation, and McCarthyite persecution. They are shut out from the press, their names are erased from its columns of print; they are buried in the most atrocious silence—which is yet another contradiction of capitalism. For it is then that the writer, poet, painter, sculptor, the creator in any field, the scientist, begins truly to live, to live on the lips of the people and in the hearts of millions of men and women throughout the world. Imperialism turns everything on its head, deforms it, diverts it into its own channels for its own profit, to multiply its dollars; whether buying the spoken word and paintings, or buying silence—stilling the expression of revolutionists, progressive individuals, those who struggle for the people and their needs.

We cannot forget, in this sad picture, the underprivileged children, the neglected, the futureless children of the Americas.

America, a continent with a high birth rate, also has a high rate of mortality. A few years ago, in 11 countries of Latin America, the death rate of children less than a year old was 125 per thousand, and in 17 others it stood at 90 per thousand. In 102 nations of the world, on the other hand, the rate is 51. In Latin America, then, 74 out of a thousand die in the first year after birth, in sadness and neglect. In some areas of Latin America that rate reaches 300 per thousand. Thousands and thousands of children up to seven years old die of incredible diseases: diarrhea, pneumonia, malnutrition, hunger. Thousands and thousands more are dying of other diseases without hospital treatment or medicines; thousands and thousands wander about, victims of endemic mental deficiency, malaria, trachoma, and other diseases caused by contamination, lack of water and other necessities.

Diseases of this nature are a chain around the necks of Latin American countries where thousands and thousands of children are dying, children of outcasts, children of the poor and of the petty bourgeoisie, with hard lives and precarious means. The statistics, which would be redundant here, are bloodcurdling. Any official publication of international organizations gathers them by the hundreds.

Regarding education, indignation swells merely thinking of what Latin America lacks on the cultural level. While the United States has a level of eight or nine years of schooling for those in its population fifteen years and older, Latin America, plundered and pauperized by the U.S., has a level of less than one year of approved schooling in the same age group.

Indignation mounts to learn that of children between five and fourteen years only 20 percent are enrolled in some countries, and in those countries with the highest level of schooling, 60 percent. That is to say, more than half the children of Latin America do not go to school. But the pain continues to grow when we learn that enrollment in the first three grades comprises more than 80 percent of those enrolled, and that in the sixth grade the enrollment fluctuates from a bare 6 to 22 pupils for each hundred who began in the first grade. Even in those countries that believe they have taken care of their children, the dropout rate between the first and sixth grade averages 73 percent. In Cuba, before the revolution, it was 74 percent. In Colombia, a "representative democracy," it is 78 percent. And if one looks closely at the countryside, in the best of cases only 1 percent of the children reach the fifth grade.

Investigating this disastrous student absenteeism, there

is one cause that explains it: the economics of poverty. Lack of schools, lack of teachers, lack of family resources, child labor. In the last analysis—imperialism and its bounty of oppression and backwardness.

To summarize this nightmare that America has lived from one end to the other: On this continent of almost 200 million human beings, two-thirds are Indians, mestizos, and Blacks—the "discriminated ones." On this continent of semicolonies, about four persons per minute die of hunger, of curable illnesses or premature old age: 5,500 per day, 2 million per year, 10 million every five years. These deaths could easily be avoided, but nevertheless they go on. Two-thirds of the Latin American population live short lives, under constant threat of death. A holocaust of lives, a holocaust that in fifteen years has caused twice the number of deaths of World War I and that continues. Meanwhile, from Latin America a continuous torrent of money flows to the United States: some $4,000 a minute, $5 million a day, $2 billion a year, $10 billion every five years. For each $1,000 that leaves us, one corpse remains. A thousand dollars per corpse: that is the price of what is called imperialism! A thousand dollars per death, four times a minute!

But why, in face of this Latin American reality, did they meet at Punta del Este? Perhaps to alleviate these ills by one small drop? No!

The people know that at Punta del Este the ministers who expelled Cuba met to renounce national sovereignty. They know that the government of the United States went there to establish not only the basis for aggression against Cuba, but also the basis for intervention against the people's liberation movement in any Latin American nation; that the United States is preparing a bloody drama for Latin America. They know that just as the exploiting oligarchies now renounce the principle of sovereignty, they will not hesitate to solicit intervention of Yankee troops against their own people. And they know that for this end the U.S. delegation proposed to establish within the Inter-American Defense Council a watchdog committee against subversion, endowed with executive powers and the authority to adopt collective measures. For the Yankee imperialists, "subversion" means the struggle of hungry people for bread, the struggle of peasants for land, the struggle of the peoples against imperialist exploitation.

A watchdog committee with executive powers within the Inter-American Defense Council means a continental repressive force against the peoples, a force under the command of the Pentagon. "Collective measures" means the landing of Yankee marines in any country of the Americas.

Revolutions are not exported, they are made by the people

To the accusation that Cuba wants to export its revolution, we reply: Revolutions are not exported, they are made by the peoples.

What Cuba can give to the peoples, and has already given, is its example.

And what does the Cuban Revolution teach? That revolution is possible, that the peoples can make it, that in the contemporary world there are no forces capable of halting the liberation movement of the people.

Our triumph would never have been feasible if the revolution itself had not been inexorably destined to arise out of existing conditions in our socioeconomic reality, a reality that exists to an even greater degree in a good number of Latin American countries.

It inevitably occurs that in the nations where the control of the Yankee monopolies is strongest, the exploitation of the oligarchy cruelest, and the situation of the laboring and peasant masses most unbearable, there too the political power appears most solid. The state of siege becomes habitual. Every manifestation of discontent by the masses is repressed by force. The democratic path is closed completely. The brutal character of dictatorship, the form of rule adopted by the ruling classes, reveals itself more clearly than ever. It is then that the revolutionary explosion of the peoples becomes inevitable.

Although it is true that in those underdeveloped countries of the Americas the working class generally is relatively small, there is a social class that, because of the subhuman conditions in which it lives, constitutes a potential force that, led by the workers and the revolutionary intellectuals, has a decisive importance in the struggle for national liberation: the peasants.

Our countries combine the circumstances of industrial underdevelopment with those of an agrarian regime of a feudal character. That is why, with all the hardships of the conditions of life of the urban workers, the rural population lives in even more horrible conditions of oppression and exploitation. But it is also, with exceptions, the absolute majority sector, at times exceeding 70 percent of the Latin American population.[13]

Discounting the landlords, who often reside in the cities, the rest of that great mass gains its livelihood working as peons on the haciendas for the most miserable wages, or works the land under conditions of exploitation that in

---

13. In 2000, close to four decades later, 77 percent of Latin America's population lived in cities.

all senses would do the Middle Ages proud. These are the circumstances that determine that in Latin America the rural poor constitute a tremendous potential revolutionary force.

The armies, the force on which the power of the exploiting classes rest, are built and equipped for conventional war. They become absolutely impotent, however, when they have to confront the irregular struggle of the peasants on their own terrain. They lose ten men for each revolutionary fighter who falls, and demoralization spreads rapidly among them from having to face an invisible enemy who does not offer them the opportunity of showing off their tactics learned in military academies, nor their swaggering—which they make such a display of in the cities to repress the workers and students.

The initial struggle by small combat units is continuously fed by new forces, the mass movement begins, and the old order little by little starts to break into a thousand pieces. That is the moment when the working class and the urban masses decide the battle.

What is it that from the beginning of the struggle of those first nuclei, makes them invincible, regardless of the numbers, power, and resources of their enemies? The support of the people. And they will be able to count on that support of the masses on an ever-increasing scale.

But the peasantry is a class that, because of the state of ignorance in which it is kept and the isolation in which it lives, needs the revolutionary and political leadership of the working class and the revolutionary intellectuals, without which it would not by itself be able to plunge into the struggle and achieve victory.

In the current historical conditions of Latin America, the national bourgeoisie cannot lead the antifeudal and anti-imperialist struggle. Experience shows that in our nations that class, even when its interests are in contradiction to those of Yankee imperialism, has been incapable of confronting it, for the national bourgeoisie is paralyzed by fear of social revolution and frightened by the cry of the exploited masses.

Fearful of social revolution, the national bourgeoisie in Latin America cannot lead the anti-imperialist struggle

Facing the dilemma of imperialism or revolution, only its most progressive layers will be with the people.

The current international relationship of forces and the worldwide movement for the liberation of the colonial and dependent peoples points out to the working class and revolutionary intellectuals of Latin America their true role, which is to place themselves resolutely in the vanguard of the struggle against imperialism and feudalism.

Imperialism, utilizing the great movie monopolies, its news services, its magazines, books, and reactionary newspapers, resorts to the most subtle lies to sow division and inculcate among the most ignorant people fear and superstition of revolutionary ideas, fear and superstition that can and should frighten only the powerful exploiters with their age-old interests and privileges.

Fostering division, a product of all kinds of prejudices, misconceptions, and lies; sectarianism, dogmatism, narrow-mindedness in analyzing the role of each social layer, its parties, organizations, and leaders—these obstruct the indispensable unity of action of the democratic and progressive forces of our peoples. They are growing pains, infantile disorders of the revolutionary movement that must be left behind. In the antifeudal and anti-imperialist struggle it is possible to organize the majority of the people around goals of liberation that bring together the working class, the peasants, the intellectual workers, the petty bourgeoisie, and the most progressive layers of the national bourgeoisie. These sectors comprise the immense majority of the population and include within its ranks great social forces capable of sweeping out imperialist domination and feudal reaction. In that broad movement they can and must struggle together for the good of their nations, for the good of their peoples, and for the good of the Americas—from the old Marxist militant, to the sincere Catholic who has nothing to do with the Yankee monopolies and the feudal lords of the land.

That movement would be capable of pulling alongside it progressive elements of the armed forces, also humiliated by the Yankee military missions, the betrayal of national interests by the feudal oligarchies, and the sacrifice of national sovereignty to Washington's dictates.

Where the roads are closed to the peoples, where the repression of workers and peasants is fierce, where the rule of the Yankee monopolies is strongest, the first and most important task is to understand that it is neither fair nor correct to beguile the peoples with the futile and conciliationist illusion of wresting power by legal means—means that do not and will not exist—from the hands of ruling classes that are entrenched in all the state positions, monopolize education, own all the means of communication, possess infinite financial resources—a power that the monopolies and oligarchies will defend by blood and fire and with the might of their police and armies.

The duty of every revolutionist is to make the revolution. It is true that the revolution will triumph in the Americas and throughout the world, but it is not for revolutionists to sit in the doorways of their houses waiting for the corpse of imperialism to pass by. The role of Job does not suit a revolutionist. Each year that the liberation of Latin America is speeded up will mean the lives of millions of children saved, millions of intellects saved for culture, an infinite quantity of pain spared the people. Even if the Yankee imperialists prepare a bloody drama for Latin America, they will not succeed in crushing the peoples' struggles; they will only arouse universal hatred against themselves. And such a drama will also mark the fall of their greedy and Stone Age system.

The duty of every revolutionist is to make the revolution

No nation in Latin America is weak—because each forms part of a family of 200 million brothers, who suffer the same miseries, who harbor the same sentiments, who have the same enemy, who dream about the same better future, and who count upon the solidarity of all honest men and women throughout the world.

Great as was the epic of Latin American independence, heroic as was that struggle, today's generation of Latin Americans is called upon to engage in an epic that is even greater and more decisive for humanity. For that struggle was for liberation from Spanish colonial power, from a decadent Spain invaded by the armies of Napoleon. Today we are called upon to struggle for liberation from the most powerful world imperialist center, from the strongest force of world imperialism, and to render humanity a service even greater than that rendered by our predecessors.

But this struggle, to a greater extent than the earlier one, will be waged by the masses, will be carried out by the people. The people are going to play a much more important role now than they did then; the leaders are and will be less important in this struggle than in the one before.

This epic before us is going to be written by the hungry Indian masses, the peasants without land, the exploited workers. It is going to be written by the progressive masses, the honest and brilliant intellectuals, who so greatly abound in our suffering Latin American lands. A struggle of masses and of ideas. An epic that will be carried forward by our peoples, mistreated and scorned by the imperialists; our people, invisible to them until today, who have begun to give them sleepless nights. Imperialism considered us a powerless and submissive flock. Now it begins to be terrified of that flock—a gigantic flock of 200 million Latin Americans in whom Yankee monopoly capitalism today sees its gravediggers.

This toiling humanity, these inhumanly exploited men and women, these paupers, controlled by the system of whip and overseer, have not counted or have counted little. From the dawn of independence their fate has been the same: Indians, gauchos, mestizos, zambos, quadroons,[14] whites without property or income, all this human mass that formed the ranks of the "nation" that was never theirs, who fell by the millions, who were cut to bits, who won independence from the mother country for the bourgeoisie, who were shut out from their share of the rewards, who

---

14. Gauchos are cattle-ranch and agricultural hands from the pampas of Argentina, Uruguay, and southern Brazil. Mestizo is the term used in Latin America to describe people of part-Indian descent; zambos, persons of mixed African and Indian descent; and quadroons, persons with one Black grandparent.

continued to occupy the lowest rung on the ladder of social benefits, continued to die of hunger, curable diseases, and neglect for lack of things that never reached them: ordinary bread, a hospital bed, medicine that cures, a helping hand.

The exploited of America have begun writing their history for themselves

But now, from one end of the continent to the other, they are signaling clearly that the hour has come: the hour of their redemption. Now this anonymous mass, this America of color, somber, taciturn America, which all over the continent sings with the same sadness and disillusionment, now this mass is beginning to enter definitively into its own history, is beginning to write it with its own blood, is beginning to suffer and die for it.

Because now in the fields and mountains of the Americas, on its hillsides, on its flatlands and in its jungles, in isolated fields and in the crush of its cities, on the banks of its great oceans and rivers, this world is beginning to tremble. Ardent fists are raised, ready to die for what is theirs, to win those rights that for five hundred years have been laughed at by one and all. Yes, now history will have to take the poor of America into account, the exploited and spurned of America, who have decided to begin writing their history for themselves for all time. Already they can be seen on the roads, on foot, day after day, in an endless march of hundreds of miles up to the "Olympian" heights of government to demand their rights.

Already they can be seen armed with stones, sticks, machetes, from one end to the other, each day, occupying lands, sinking stakes into the land that belongs to them and defending it with their lives. They can be seen carrying signs, slogans, banners; unfurling them in the mountain and prairie winds. And the wave of trembling anger, of demands for justice, of claims for rights trampled underfoot, which is beginning to sweep the lands of Latin America, will not stop. That wave will swell with each passing day. For that wave is composed of the greatest number, the majorities in every respect, those whose labor amasses the wealth and creates all value, those who turn the wheels of history. Now they are awakening from the long, brutalizing sleep to which they had been subjected.

For this great mass of humanity has said, "Enough!" and has begun to march. And their march of giants will not be halted until they conquer true independence—for which they have died in vain more than once. Today, however, those who die will die as in Cuba, as at Playa Girón: they will die for their one, true, never-to-be-surrendered independence.

Patria o muerte!
Venceremos!

THE PEOPLE OF CUBA
Havana, Cuba
Free Territory of the Americas
February 4, 1962

The National General Assembly of the Cuban People resolves that this Declaration be known as the Second Declaration of Havana, translated into the major languages, and distributed throughout the world. It also resolves to urge all friends of the Cuban Revolution in Latin America to distribute it widely among the masses of workers, peasants, students, and intellectuals of this continent.

Chronology *and* Glossary

March and rally of 100,000 in Santiago de Cuba, February 10, 1962.
Numerous such actions were organized across Cuba in support of the
Second Declaration of Havana.

CHRONOLOGY

1952

March 10 — Former Cuban president and military strongman Fulgencio Batista organizes coup d'état, ousting elected government of Carlos Prío. Batista establishes an increasingly brutal military dictatorship closely allied with many of the country's wealthiest families and U.S. business interests in Cuba, and supported by Washington.

April 9 — Revolutionary upsurge in Bolivia topples military dictatorship and installs bourgeois government. The armed uprising is led by tin miners in vanguard of a trade union movement allied with peasant organizations. The largest tin mines are nationalized, unions are legalized, land reform initiated, and a literacy requirement effectively denying the ballot to Bolivia's indigenous majority abolished.

1953

July 26 — Aiming to initiate insurrection against Batista tyranny, some 160 revolutionaries organized and led by Fidel Castro launch attack on Moncada army garrison in Santiago de Cuba and garrison in nearby Bayamo. Combatants fail to take either military headquarters, and over 50 captured revolutionaries are murdered. Castro and 27 other fighters are subsequently captured, tried, and sentenced to up to 15 years in prison.

July 27 — Armistice ends three-year-long Korean War. Korean workers and peasants and Chinese People's Liberation Army inflict first military defeat on U.S. imperialism, blocking

Washington from toppling government in north Korea and attacking workers and peasants regime in China.

1954

May 7 — French forces surrender to Communist-led Vietnamese liberation fighters at Dien Bien Phu, signaling defeat of French colonialism in Indochina. At conference in Geneva, Moscow backs U.S., British, and French imperialist proposal to partition Vietnam. A U.S.-backed regime is imposed in south.

June–September — Seeking to crush worker, peasant, and student struggles in Guatemala and turn back initial steps toward land reform, mercenary forces backed by CIA invade country in order to oust government of Jacobo Arbenz. Rejecting popular demands to arm population to resist, Arbenz resigns June 27 and soon flees country. Rightist forces organized and backed by CIA enter Guatemala City in August.

October 31 — Algerian war for independence begins, as fighters organized by National Liberation Front (FLN) challenge French colonial rule.

1955

May 15 — Following a nationwide amnesty campaign, Fidel Castro and the other imprisoned Moncadistas are freed. Within weeks Castro leads unification of several revolutionary organizations to form July 26 Revolutionary Movement. In July he and others leave for Mexico, where they prepare to relaunch revolutionary armed struggle against Batista tyranny.

December 5 — Bus boycott begins in Montgomery, Alabama, announcing opening of mass proletarian-based movement led by Blacks to bring down "Jim Crow" racial segregation across U.S. South. The boycott ends over a year later, with elimination of policies forcing Blacks to move to the back of the bus.

1956

July–December — In face of mounting anti-imperialist sentiment and actions in Egypt, government of Gamal Abdel Nasser nationalizes Suez Canal, largely owned and controlled by British and French capital. Asserting U.S. dominance in Mideast at expense of former European powers, Washington condemns military intervention in Egypt by British, French, and Israeli troops, forcing withdrawal.

December 2 — Eighty-two members of July 26 Movement, including Moncadistas Fidel Castro, Raúl Castro, and Juan Almeida, and the Argentine doctor Ernesto Che Guevara, land in Cuba from Mexico aboard the yacht *Granma* to initiate revolutionary war. Rebel Army is born.

1957

September — In face of 1954 Supreme Court decision barring racial segregation of schools, Central High School in Little Rock, Arkansas, admits nine Black students. Governor of Arkansas unleashes racist mobs to assault Black youth. As international outrage mounts, U.S. president Dwight Eisenhower bends to growing pressure at home and abroad to respond to call by supporters of Black rights, sending in federal troops to protect students.

December 14 — On behalf of July 26 Movement, Fidel Castro repudiates Miami Pact, an attempt by bourgeois opposition forces to take leadership of anti-Batista struggle.

1958

January 23 — Popular rebellion in Caracas overthrows regime of Venezuelan dictator Marcos Pérez Jiménez.

May — Demonstrations in Argentina, Paraguay, Bolivia, Peru, Venezuela, and other countries protest tour of Latin America by U.S. vice president Richard Nixon and denounce U.S. domination of region.

July — Batista military offensive against Rebel Army command center in Sierra Maestra mountains is defeated, opening way for revolutionary forces to drive across island to final victory.

1959

January 1 — Triumph of revolutionary war. In face of Rebel Army advances and broadening popular insurrection and general strike led by July 26 Movement, Batista flees Cuba. Over next few days Rebel Army takes control of all military garrisons and police headquarters. Former judge Manuel Urrutia becomes president. July 26 Movement cadres head several ministries, initially as minority in new government.

February 16 — Revolutionary mobilizations of workers and peasants deepen, leading to resignation of Prime Minister José Miró Cardona. Fidel Castro becomes prime minister.

March 6 — Cuba's revolutionary government approves law imposing rent reduction of 30–50 percent.

March 22 — Fidel Castro announces measures to outlaw racial discrimination in all public facilities and in employment.

May 17 — Cuban government signs first agrarian reform law, limiting size of private landholdings to 1,000 acres. Mass mobilizations of peasants and workers confiscate landed estates of foreign and Cuban owners who exceed limit. Land titles are distributed to 100,000 landless peasants.

July 16–17 — In face of Urrutia's opposition to revolution's measures, Fidel Castro resigns as prime minister. A massive popular outpouring forces Urrutia to resign, and he is replaced as president by July 26 Movement cadre Osvaldo Dorticós. Castro resumes responsibilities as prime minister on July 26.

July — Civil war breaks out in Laos between Pathet Lao liberation front and U.S.-backed proimperialist forces.

November 1 — Some 2,000 Panamanian workers and students cross into Canal Zone to plant Panamanian flag. Tear-gassing and assaults by club-wielding U.S. forces spark further protests demanding Panama's sovereignty over canal.

November 26 — Che Guevara becomes head of National Bank, replacing Felipe Pazos, one of last bourgeois representatives in the government.

1960

February 1 — Sit-in by Black students at whites-only lunch counter at Woolworth's department store in Greensboro, North Carolina, opens wave of sit-ins across U.S. South demanding desegregation of public facilities.

March 4 — *La Coubre*, French ship carrying Belgian arms bought by Cubans for their defense, explodes in Havana harbor, killing 101 people.

June 29–July 1 — Oil workers backed by revolutionary government take over Texaco, Esso, and Shell refineries following refusals to refine petroleum bought by Cuba from Soviet Union.

June 30 — Congo wins independence from Belgium. Patrice Lumumba becomes prime minister.

July 6 — U.S. president Dwight Eisenhower, as punitive measure, orders sugar imports Washington had agreed to buy from Cuba reduced by 700,000 tons, slashing sugar quota for the remainder of 1960 by 95 percent.

July 9 — Soviet Union announces it will purchase all Cuban sugar the U.S. refuses to buy.

July 26–August 8 — First Latin American Youth Congress in Cuba is attended by nearly 1,000 young people from every Latin American nation, as well as United States, Canada, Soviet Union, and other countries. Many participants are won to perspective of emulating Cuban revolutionists' example.

August 6 — In face of increasing U.S. economic aggression and sabotage, Cuba's revolutionary government responds to workers' initiatives and decrees nationalization of major U.S. companies. As workers mobilize across island to combat economic disruption by capitalists, virtually all large-scale Cuban-owned industry is nationalized by end of October.

August 22–29 — Organization of American States (OAS) holds foreign ministers meeting in San José, Costa Rica, which issues

Declaration of San José condemning Cuba's revolutionary course. The OAS includes every Latin American country except those that remain colonies plus the United States.

September 2 — One million Cubans, constituting themselves the National General Assembly of the Cuban People, condemn OAS Declaration of San José and adopt First Declaration of Havana.

September 26 — Fidel Castro, addressing UN General Assembly, denounces U.S. attacks on Cuba and declares solidarity with struggle against imperialism worldwide.

October 13 — All foreign (except Canadian-owned) and Cuban banks are nationalized, as are 382 large Cuban-owned companies.

October 14 — Urban Reform Law enacted, barring landlords from renting out urban real estate. Under law most Cubans become owners of their homes, with others paying maximum rent to state of 10 percent of family income.

Late December — Revolutionary militias mobilize in response to U.S. military threats against Cuba made during its final days by Eisenhower administration.

1961

January 1 — "Year of Education" begins in Cuba. In a year-long literacy campaign, more than 100,000 teachers, overwhelmingly youth and students, fan out to every corner of the island. By end of effort, nearly one million workers and peasants of all ages had learned to read and write. The nationwide mobilization wipes out illiteracy.

January 3 — Washington breaks diplomatic relations with Cuba.

January 16 — State Department announces that U.S. citizens traveling to Cuba must obtain specific authorization.

January 17 — Patrice Lumumba, ousted as prime minister of Congo in September 1960 coup, is murdered on orders of Joseph Mobutu, with direct participation of Belgian officials and backing by Washington.

March 31 — U.S. president John F. Kennedy halts all remaining sugar imports from Cuba.

April 17–19 — U.S.-organized mercenary invasion is defeated in less than 72 hours at Playa Girón on Bay of Pigs by Cuba's Revolutionary Armed Forces, Revolutionary National Police, and popular militias. On eve of attack, Fidel Castro for first time explains socialist course of revolution at mass rally in Havana mobilizing Cuban people to face impending invasion. Victory of Cuban defenders in crushing mercenaries marks U.S. imperialism's first military defeat in Latin America.

May 4 — First Freedom Ride occurs in U.S. South, as activists take buses across state borders in attempt to desegregate interstate public transportation.

May 31 — Rafael Trujillo, longtime dictator of Dominican Republic, is assassinated. His protegé Joaquín Balaguer, the country's president, assumes full control, with U.S. backing.

August 5–17 — At meeting of OAS Economic and Social Conference in Punta del Este, Uruguay, U.S. government announces "Alliance for Progress," aimed at propping up compliant capitalist regimes and enriching U.S. bankers and investors. Plan allocates $20 billion in loans over ten years to Latin American regimes in exchange for cooperation in opposing Cuba's revolutionary government. Che Guevara, at head of Cuba's delegation, uses meeting as platform to expose character of imperialist-dominated "Alliance" and mobilize opposition to it.

August 30 — President Kennedy orders 148,000 National Guard and reserve troops to active duty during Berlin crisis, in which U.S. and Soviet military forces face off.

November — Amid a growing popular rebellion in Dominican Republic, Washington deploys warships off Dominican coast to bolster Balaguer regime.

December — Cuban ship *Bahía de Nipe* leaves Havana for North Africa, carrying weapons and ammunition to aid Algerian National Liberation Front's (FLN) fight to overturn French colonial rule. Ship returns in January with 76 wounded

Algerian fighters and 20 war orphans.

December 2 — Announcing unification of July 26 Movement with Popular Socialist Party and Revolutionary Directorate, Fidel Castro delivers speech, "I Will Be a Marxist-Leninist to the End of My Life."

1962

January 22–31 — Meeting of foreign ministers of Latin America and U.S. sponsored by OAS in Punta del Este, Uruguay, expels Cuba from OAS and supports military moves against it. Cuba's delegation, headed by President Osvaldo Dorticós, uses meeting as platform to condemn imperialist exploitation of Latin America.

February 3 — President Kennedy orders total embargo on U.S. trade with Cuba.

February 4 — National General Assembly of one million in Havana's Plaza of the Revolution adopts Second Declaration of Havana, proclaiming Cuba's support to revolutionary struggle for popular power throughout Americas.

July 3 — Following eight-year national liberation struggle, Algeria wins independence from France. Workers and peasants government led by Ahmed Ben Bella establishes close ties with revolutionary Cuban government.

October 22–28 — Kennedy administration orders naval blockade of Cuba, places U.S. armed forces on nuclear alert, and demands removal from island of Soviet-supplied nuclear missile defense. Missiles had been installed following a mutual defense agreement between Cuba and Soviet Union in face of Washington's preparations to invade Cuba. In response to U.S. aggression, millions of Cubans mobilize to defend the socialist revolution, pushing back U.S. nuclear threats. Following exchange between U.S. and Soviet governments, Premier Nikita Khrushchev, without consulting Cuban government, announces removal of missiles.

1963

April–May — Black rights fighters in Birmingham, Alabama, conduct mass marches and sit-ins to desegregate public facilities. As they defend themselves against brutal assaults by cops employing billy clubs, dogs, fire hoses, and tear gas, the events become known as "The Battle of Birmingham."

May 24 — Algeria welcomes fifty-five Cuban volunteer doctors, dentists, nurses, and other medical personnel, the first such internationalist mission of the Cuban Revolution.

August 28 — March on Washington for Jobs and Freedom draws 250,000 people demanding civil rights. Coinciding with march, a call for a break with the Democratic Party and formation of a Freedom Now Party is issued, with support of a number of figures in Black rights struggle, as well as Nation of Islam.

October 3 — Cuba enacts second agrarian reform, confiscating private holdings in excess of 165 acres. Property is seized from some 10,000 capitalist farmers who own 20 percent of Cuba's agricultural land and constitute a base for counterrevolutionary activity organized by Washington. Measure brings social relations on land in harmony with state ownership of industry, strengthening worker-farmer alliance.

October 22 — Battalion of almost 700 Cuban volunteer troops arrives in Algeria to defend newly independent revolutionary regime against imperialist-inspired attacks by Morocco.

1964

January 9 — U.S. troops kill some twenty Panamanians and wound hundreds during protests against refusal of U.S. officials to fly Panamanian flag wherever U.S. flag is displayed. Over following week, thousands of Panamanians mobilize to demand sovereignty over Panama Canal.

March 31–April 2 — U.S.-backed military coup in Brazil overthrows elected government of João Goulart, inaugurating years of bloody terror.

June–August — Thousands of youth participate in "Freedom Summer" to register Blacks to vote in U.S. South. On June 21 three volunteers—James Chaney, Andrew Goodman, and Michael Schwerner—are murdered in Mississippi by Ku Klux Klan gang led by local deputy sheriff.

August — Using an alleged naval incident in waters off Indochina as pretext, U.S. Congress passes Tonkin Gulf resolution. Bombing of North Vietnam and rapid escalation of war against Vietnamese liberation forces begins. By 1969 some 540,000 U.S. troops are fighting in Vietnam.

December 11 — Che Guevara addresses UN General Assembly. Citing the revolutionary perspective of Second Declaration of Havana, he affirms Cuba's solidarity with worldwide fight against imperialist exploitation.

1965

February 21 — Malcolm X, revolutionary leader of struggle for Black liberation and against U.S. imperialist oppression and exploitation of working people the world over, is assassinated in New York City.

March 13 — Condemning split between the governing parties of Soviet Union and China, Fidel Castro declares that "Division in the face of the enemy was never a revolutionary or intelligent strategy" and calls for united front to defend Vietnam from U.S. imperialist attack.

April 1 — Che Guevara delivers farewell letter to Fidel Castro resigning leadership duties in Cuba in order to freely participate in revolutionary struggles abroad. While awaiting preparations for revolutionary front in South America's Southern Cone, he goes to Congo at head of column of more than 100 Cuban volunteers assisting popular forces fighting that country's proimperialist regime. A second column of Cuban volunteers goes to Congo-Brazzaville to constitute a reserve force and to aid independence fighters in Angola.

April 17 — 20,000 march in first nationwide demonstration in Washington, D.C., to protest U.S. war in Vietnam. Initiated by Students for a Democratic Society (SDS), it is organized as a united-front action together with Young Socialist Alliance, W.E.B. DuBois Clubs, and others.

April 28 — Some 24,000 U.S. troops invade the Dominican Republic to crush popular uprising against Washington-backed military junta.

June 19 — Revolutionary government in Algeria led by Ben Bella is overthrown in military coup.

August — Rebellion by Black community drives police out of Watts neighborhood of Los Angeles. Some 13,000 National Guardsmen assault Blacks in area, leaving 36 dead, 900 injured, and 4,000 arrested. First of numerous explosions by Blacks in major U.S. cities over next three years.

October 3 — During public meeting to introduce Central Committee of newly founded Communist Party of Cuba, Fidel Castro reads Che Guevara's April 1 letter announcing plans to join struggles against imperialist exploitation in other parts of the world.

1966

January 3–14 — Tricontinental Conference of Solidarity of the Peoples of Asia, Africa, and Latin America is held in Havana, attended by anti-imperialist fighters from around world.

November — Che Guevara arrives in Bolivia to lead a revolutionary front in South America's Southern Cone. Guevara is wounded and captured October 8, 1967, in a CIA-organized operation by Bolivian troops. He is murdered the following day by Bolivian armed forces after consultation with Washington.

1967

July 31–August 10 — Organization of Latin American Solidarity (OLAS) conference is held in Havana, attended by revolutionary forces and left political parties from throughout the Americas, including the United States. Under banner citing Second Declaration of Havana's call to action—"The duty of every revolutionist is to make the revolution"— the conference proclaims support for popular struggles throughout Latin America.

GLOSSARY

Antilles – The islands of the Caribbean, including Cuba.

Balaguer, Joaquín (1907–2002) – High official in Trujillo dictatorship in Dominican Republic. U.S.-backed president, 1960–62, 1966–78, and 1986–96.

Barnes, Jack (1940–) – National secretary of Socialist Workers Party (SWP) in United States since 1972. Participated in First Latin American Youth Congress in Cuba in summer 1960. Joined Young Socialist Alliance in 1960 and SWP in 1961. Author of numerous books, pamphlets, and articles on communist politics, strategy, and organization. Member of editorial board of *New International* magazine.

Batista, Fulgencio (1901–1973) – Military strongman in Cuba 1934–44. Led coup on March 10, 1952, establishing military-police tyranny. Fled Cuba January 1, 1959, in face of advancing Rebel Army and popular insurrection.

Bolívar, Simón (1783–1830) – Latin American patriot, born in Caracas, known as The Liberator. Led series of armed rebellions 1810–24 that helped win independence from Spain for much of Latin America.

Bruno, Giordano (1548–1600) – Italian philosopher, astronomer, and mathematician. Burned at stake for heresy by Roman Catholic hierarchy.

Castro, Fidel (1926–) – Organized and led revolutionary movement against Batista tyranny that carried out July 26, 1953, attack on Moncada garrison in Santiago de Cuba and Carlos Manuel de Céspedes garrison in Bayamo. Captured, tried, and sentenced to fifteen years in prison. Released in 1955 after national amnesty campaign, he led founding of July 26 Revolutionary Movement. Organized *Granma* expedition from Mexico, to launch revolutionary war in Cuba, late 1956. Commander of Rebel Army from founding, 1956–58. Following revolution's triumph, was Cuba's prime minister from February 1959 to 1976. Has been president of Council of State and of Council of Ministers since 1976, as well as commander in chief of Revolutionary Armed Forces, and, since its founding in 1965, first secretary of the Communist Party of Cuba.

CENTO (Central Treaty Organization) – Military alliance of Turkey, Iran, Pakistan, and United Kingdom, 1955–79, formed at urging of British and U.S. governments to counter Soviet Union's influence in Mideast. U.S. became associate member in 1959. Dissolved following Iranian Revolution of 1979.

Diderot, Denis (1713–1784) – French writer and philosopher of the Enlightenment.

Engels, Frederick (1820–1895) – Lifelong collaborator of Karl Marx and cofounder with him of modern communist workers movement.

Guevara, Ernesto Che (1928–1967) – Argentine-born leader of Cuban Revolution. Recruited in Mexico in 1955 to *Granma* expedition as troop doctor. First Rebel Army combatant promoted to commander, 1957. After 1959 triumph held responsibilities that included head of National Bank and minister of industry. Led Cuban column fighting alongside anti-imperialist forces in Congo 1965. Led detachment of internationalist volunteers to Bolivia 1966–67. Wounded and captured by Bolivian army during CIA-organized counterguerrilla operation, October 8, 1967. Murdered the following day.

Hidalgo, Miguel (1753–1811) – Known as father of Mexico's independence, led 1810 independence uprising against Spanish rule. Captured and shot. A Catholic priest.

Hus, Jan (1370–1415) – Czech religious reformer. Condemned for heresy and burned at stake by Roman Catholic hierarchy.

Inquisitors – Officials of church courts set up in late Middle Ages to enforce allegiance to Roman Catholic religious dogma and the church hierarchy, which constituted a central pillar of the feudal order threatened by rising capitalist social relations and bourgeois political forces. Inquisition reached its peak in late 15th and early 16th centuries in Spain, where some 2,000 were burned at the stake as heretics.

Juárez, Benito (1806–1872) – President of Mexico 1861–72, who fought French occupation of country (1864–67). Mexico's national hero.

July 26 Revolutionary Movement – Founded June 1955 by Fidel Castro and other participants in Moncada attack, together with other revolutionary forces. During war against tyranny was composed of Rebel Army in mountains (*Sierra*) and underground network in cities and countryside (*Llano*—"plains"). In May 1958 national leadership was centralized in Sierra Maestra; Fidel Castro was chosen general secretary. Led fusion with Popular Socialist Party and Revolutionary Directorate in 1961.

Lenin, V.I. (1870–1924) – Founder of Bolshevik Party. Central leader of 1917 October Revolution in Russia. Chair of Council of People's Commissars (Soviet government) 1917–24; member of Executive Committee of Communist International 1919–24.

Martí, José (1853–1895) – Cuba's national hero. A noted revolutionary, poet, writer, speaker, journalist, and combatant. Founded Cuban Revolutionary Party in 1892 to fight Spanish colonial rule and oppose U.S. designs on Cuba. Organized and planned 1895 independence war. Killed in battle with Spanish troops at Dos Ríos in Oriente province. His anti-imperialist program and broader revolutionary writings are at center of Cuba's internationalist traditions and revolutionary political heritage.

Marx, Karl (1818–1883) – Founder with Frederick Engels of modern communist workers movement and architect of its programmatic foundations.

McCarthy, Joseph (1908–1957) – Republican senator from Wisconsin. Most prominent U.S. anticommunist witch-hunter of early 1950s.

Monroe Doctrine – Policy enunciated in 1823 by President James Monroe (1758–1831). Doctrine outlined government policy of nascent U.S. bourgeoisie to protect the young republic against counterrevolutionary policies of powerful European monarchies, especially United Kingdom and France, warning them to stay out of the affairs of the Americas. From closing decade of nineteenth century onward, as U.S. became imperialist world power, Monroe Doctrine was transformed into justification for U.S. political and military intervention against nations of Latin America and Caribbean trying to break stranglehold of U.S. domination.

Napoleon I (Napoleon Bonaparte) (1769–1821) – Leading general in revolutionary wars that defended conquests of French Revolution. In 1799, as the revolution retreated, led coup d'état, naming himself First Consul and, from 1804 to 1815, emperor of France. Both the revolutionary wars and later dynastic wars against a reactionary coalition of British, Prussian, Russian and Austrian monarchies dealt blows to remaining feudal relations in Germany and across western Europe.

NATO (North Atlantic Treaty Organization) – Military alliance, formed 1949, of U.S., Canada, and Western European powers to oppose Soviet Union and Central and Eastern European governments allied with USSR.

O'Higgins, Bernardo (1778–1842) – Commanded military forces that won Chile's independence from Spain in 1818. First Chilean head of state.

Oppenheimer, J. Robert (1904–1967) – U.S. physicist; director of project that developed atomic bomb 1943–45. Accused of Communist sympathies during early 1950s, leading to removal of his security clearance.

Platt Amendment – Drafted by U.S. Sen. Orville Platt (1827–1905) as rider to Army Appropriations Bill of 1901, subsequently incorporated as amendment to Cuban constitution. Granted Washington the right to intervene in Cuban affairs at any time and establish military bases on Cuban soil. Abrogated in May 1934 under treaty signed by the government in Havana and Franklin Delano Roosevelt administration in U.S.; treaty at the same time legalized all other concessions granted by Cuba during U.S. occupation, including control in perpetuity of Guantánamo naval base.

Popular Socialist Party (PSP) – Name taken in 1944 by Communist Party of Cuba imposed as part of worldwide Popular Front and "national unity" policies. Rejected dictatorship imposed by Batista after 1952 coup but opposed revolutionary political course of July 26 Movement. PSP collaborated with July 26 Movement in final months of struggle to topple dictatorship. Fused with July 26 Movement and Revolutionary Directorate in 1961.

Revolutionary Directorate – Formed in 1955 by José Antonio Echeverría and other leaders of Federation of University Students. Organized March 13, 1957, attack on Presidential Palace during and immediately after which a number of its central leaders were killed. In early 1958 it organized guerrilla column in Escambray mountains of Las Villas, which later became part of front commanded by Che Guevara. Fused with July 26 Movement and Popular Socialist Party in 1961.

Robeson, Paul (1898–1976) – U.S. singer and actor. A target of government anticommunist witch-hunt, his passport was revoked in 1950.

Rosenberg, Julius (1918–1953) and **Ethel** (1915–1953) – Members of U.S. Communist Party framed up for conspiracy to commit espionage for Soviet Union and executed.

Rousseau, Jean-Jacques (1712–1778) – French philosopher and writer, whose writings influenced leaders of French Revolution.

Sandino, Augusto César (1895–1934) – Led six-year guerrilla struggle in Nicaragua against U.S. Marines and proimperialist forces 1927–33. Murdered on orders of U.S.-backed dictator Anastasio Somoza.

San Martín, José de (1778–1850) – Argentine political leader who commanded forces that helped win independence of Argentina, Chile, and Peru from Spain.

SEATO (Southeast Asia Treaty Organization) – U.S.-led military alliance, 1955–77, formed to combat "communist expansionism." Participating were several imperialist governments—the U.S., Australia, France, New Zealand, and United Kingdom—as well as Pakistan, Philippines, and Thailand.

Sucre, Antonio José de (1795–1830) – Leader of Latin American revolt against Spanish rule that in 1822 liberated what is now Ecuador and ousted Spanish troops from Bolivia (1825).

Tiradentes (Joaquim José da Silva Xavier) (1748–1792) – Led unsuccessful revolt against Portuguese rule in Brazil, for which he was hanged. A physician and dentist, he was popularly known as "Tiradentes" (tooth-puller).

Trujillo, Rafael Leónidas (1891–1961) – Dictator in Dominican Republic from 1930 until his death. After 1959, backed by Washington, he organized attacks against Cuban Revolution. Assassinated May 30, 1961, by high-ranking officials of Dominican military with at least tacit support of Washington.

Voltaire (François-Marie Arouet) (1694–1778) – French satirist and historian of the Enlightenment.

Zapata, Emiliano (1879–1919) – A leader of 1910 Mexican Revolution. Organized and led a peasant army that fought for "land and liberty."

INDEX

Agrarian reform, 54; in Cuba, 13–14, 58, 82, 87
Algeria, 17, 80, 85–86, 87, 89
Alliance for Progress, 60–61, 63, 85
Almeida, Juan, 81
Anticommunism, 47, 65
Arbenz, Jacobo, 80
Argentina, 61

Bacardi rum, 13
Balaguer, Joaquín, 50–51, 85, 91
Barnes, Jack, 10, 91
Batista, Fulgencio, 79, 82, 91
Bay of Pigs. *See* Playa Girón
Ben Bella, Ahmed, 86, 89
Berlin crisis (1961), 58, 85
Birmingham, Battle of (1963), 87
Blacks: in Cuba, 58–59, 82; in Latin America, 9, 20, 30, 31, 62, 74, 75; in U.S., 20–21, 27, 29, 62–63, 87, 88, 89. *See also* United States, civil rights movement in
Bolívar, Simón, 26, 53, 91
Bolivia, 61, 79, 89
Brazil, 61, 87
Bruno, Giordano, 47, 91

Capitalism, 11; and bourgeois revolutions, 40–41, 46, 47; contradictions of, 43–44; and national bourgeoisies, 9, 11, 20, 70–71, 72; rise of, 39–42, 43; working class as gravediggers of, 43, 74. *See also* Imperialism; U.S. imperialism

Castro, Fidel, 16, 79, 80, 81, 82, 84, 86, 88, 91–92; and Declarations of Havana, 12, 17–18, 20
Castro, Raúl, 81
CENTO (Central Treaty Organization), 58, 92
Central Intelligence Agency (CIA), 49, 50
Chaney, James, 88
China, 15–16, 28, 29, 79–80, 88
Christians, early, 46, 47
Church hierarchy, 46, 92–93
Colombia, 66
Colonialism, 44; Spanish, 49, 73, 93; worldwide struggle against, 44, 48, 71. *See also* Imperialism
Communist International, 10
Communist Manifesto, 11
Communist Parties, Latin American, 19–20, 72
Congo, 83, 84, 88
Cuba: anti-Batista struggle in, 28, 79, 81, 82; expelled from OAS, 52–53, 59, 67, 85; fight for sovereignty, 25, 26–27, 37–39, 54, 59; imperialist exploitation of, 26, 37–38, 59, 66; internationalist solidarity of, 17, 31–32, 85–86, 87; literacy drive in, 17, 55, 84; nationalizations of capitalist property, 12–13, 16, 58, 83, 84; revolutionary example of, 14, 19–20, 38–39, 45–46, 54–55, 68, 83; social measures of revolution, 13–14, 16, 17, 54, 58–59, 82, 83, 84, 87; solidar-

Our History Is Still Being Written

THE STORY OF THREE CHINESE-CUBAN GENERALS IN THE CUBAN REVOLUTION

ARMANDO CHOY, GUSTAVO CHUI, AND MOISÉS SÍO WONG talk about the historic place of Chinese immigration to Cuba, as well as over five decades of revolutionary action and internationalism, from Cuba to Angola and Venezuela today. Through their stories we see the social and political forces that gave birth to the Cuban nation and opened the door to socialist revolution in the Americas. 37 pages of photos and illustrations, plus glossary and index. Edited with an introduction by Mary-Alice Waters. Also in Spanish. $20

"… Illustrated by contemporary photos, it has vigor and vividness …
Puts across an idealism badly needed in a world of materialistic pursuits.
The book may be a history 'still being written' as the title suggests,
[but] it has already struck a chord with me."

—LI ANSHAN, PEKING UNIVERSITY
JOURNAL OF CHINESE OVERSEAS, NOVEMBER 2006

"… Original perspectives on and from the Chinese-
Cuban community."
—MULTICULTURAL REVIEW, FALL 2006

"Their stories cover not only the excitement of fifty
years ago, but also the years since … [a] valuable
look at the evolution of modern Cuban history …"
—MIDWEST BOOK REVIEW, MARCH 2006

To Speak the Truth

Why Washington's 'Cold War' against Cuba Doesn't End

FIDEL CASTRO, ERNESTO CHE GUEVARA

In historic speeches before the United Nations and UN bodies, Guevara and Castro address the peoples of the world, explaining why the U.S. government so fears the example set by the socialist revolution in Cuba and why Washington's effort to destroy it will fail. $17

Playa Girón/Bay of Pigs

Washington's First Military Defeat in the Americas

FIDEL CASTRO, JOSÉ RAMÓN FERNÁNDEZ

In fewer than 72 hours of combat in April 1961, Cuba's revolutionary armed forces defeated a U.S.-organized invasion by 1,500 mercenaries. In the process, the Cuban people set an example for workers, farmers, and youth the world over that with political consciousness, class solidarity, courage, and revolutionary leadership, one can stand up to enormous might and seemingly insurmountable odds—and win. Also in Spanish. $20

From the Escambray to the Congo

In the Whirlwind of the Cuban Revolution

VÍCTOR DREKE

The author describes how easy it became after the Cuban Revolution to take down a rope segregating blacks from whites in the town square, yet how enormous was the battle to transform social relations underlying all the "ropes" inherited from capitalism and Yankee domination. Dreke, second in command of the internationalist column in the Congo led by Che Guevara in 1965, recounts the creative joy with which working people have defended their revolutionary course—from Cuba's Escambray mountains to Africa and beyond. Also in Spanish. $17

www.pathfinderpress.com

Cuba and the Coming American Revolution

JACK BARNES

"There will be a victorious revolution in the United States before there will be a victorious counterrevolution in Cuba." That 1961 statement by Fidel Castro remains as true today as when it was spoken. This is a book about the class struggle in the U.S., where the revolutionary capacities of workers and farmers are today as utterly discounted by the ruling powers as were those of the Cuban toilers. Also in Spanish and French. $13

Che Guevara Talks to Young People

ERNESTO CHE GUEVARA

In eight talks from 1959 to 1964, the Argentine-born revolutionary challenges youth of Cuba and the world to study, to work, to become disciplined. To join the front lines of struggles, small and large. To politicize their organizations and themselves. To become a different kind of human being as they strive together with working people of all lands to transform the world. Also in Spanish. $15

Pombo: A Man of Che's 'guerrilla'

With Che Guevara in Bolivia, 1966–68

HARRY VILLEGAS

A firsthand account of the 1966–68 revolutionary campaign in Bolivia led by Ernesto Che Guevara. This is the story of Pombo—the nom de guerre of Harry Villegas, a young fighter still in his 20s, who was a member of Guevara's general staff. Villegas led the small group of combatants who survived the Bolivian army's encirclement and lived to recount this epic chapter in the history of the Americas. $23

Dynamics of the Cuban Revolution

A Marxist Appreciation

JOSEPH HANSEN

How did the Cuban Revolution unfold? Why does it represent an "unbearable challenge" to U.S. imperialism? What political obstacles has it overcome? Written as the revolution advanced from its earliest days. $25

Also from
PATHFINDER

The Changing Face of U.S. Politics
Working-Class Politics and the Trade Unions
JACK BARNES

Building the kind of party working people need to prepare for coming class battles through which they will organize and strengthen the unions, as they revolutionize themselves and all society. A handbook for those repelled by the class inequalities, racism, women's oppression, cop violence, and wars inherent in capitalism, for those who are seeking the road toward effective action to overturn that exploitative system and join in reconstructing the world on new, socialist foundations. $23. Also in Spanish, French, and Swedish.

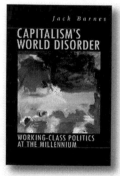

Capitalism's World Disorder
Working-Class Politics at the Millennium
JACK BARNES

The social devastation and financial panic, the coarsening of politics, the cop brutality and acts of imperialist aggression accelerating around us—all are the product not of something gone wrong with capitalism but of its lawful workings. Yet the future can be changed by the united struggle and selfless action of workers and farmers conscious of their power to transform the world. $24. Also in Spanish and French.

The Communist Manifesto
KARL MARX AND FREDERICK ENGELS
Founding document of the modern working-class movement, published in 1848. Explains why communism is not a set of preconceived principles but the line of march of the working class toward power, "springing from an existing class struggle, a historical movement going on under our very eyes." $4. Also in Spanish.

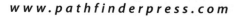

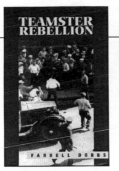

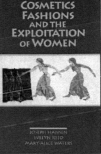

Teamster Rebellion

FARRELL DOBBS

The 1934 strikes that built the industrial union movement in Minneapolis and helped pave the way for the CIO, recounted by a central leader of that battle. The first in a four-volume series on the class-struggle leadership of the strikes and organizing drives that transformed the Teamsters union in much of the Midwest into a fighting social movement and pointed the road toward independent labor political action. $19. Also in Spanish.

Thomas Sankara Speaks

The Burkina Faso Revolution, 1983–87

Colonialism and imperialist domination have left a legacy of hunger, illiteracy, and economic backwardness in Africa. In 1983 the peasants and workers of Burkina Faso established a popular revolutionary government and began to combat the causes of such devastation. Thomas Sankara, who led that struggle, explains the example set for Africa and the world. $23

Cosmetics, Fashions, and the Exploitation of Women

JOSEPH HANSEN, EVELYN REED, MARY-ALICE WATERS

How big business plays on women's second-class status and social insecurities to market cosmetics and rake in profits. The introduction by Mary-Alice Waters explains how the entry of millions of women into the workforce during and after World War II irreversibly changed U.S. society and laid the basis for a renewed rise of struggles for women's emancipation. $15

The Struggle against Fascism in Germany

LEON TROTSKY

Writing in the heat of struggle against the rising Nazi movement, a central leader of the Russian Revolution examines the class roots of fascism and advances a revolutionary strategy to combat and defeat it. $32

America's Revolutionary Heritage

EDITED BY GEORGE NOVACK

A historical materialist analysis of the genocide against Native Americans, the American Revolution, the Civil War, the rise of industrial capitalism, and the first wave of the fight for women's rights. $22.95

Their Trotsky and Ours

JACK BARNES

To lead the working class in a successful revolution, a mass proletarian party is needed whose cadres, well beforehand, have absorbed a world communist program, are proletarian in life and work, derive deep satisfaction from doing politics, and have forged a leadership with an acute sense of what to do next. This book is about building such a party. $15. Also in Spanish and French.

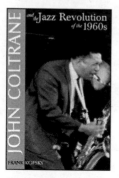

John Coltrane
and the Jazz Revolution of the 1960s

FRANK KOFSKY

John Coltrane's role in spearheading innovations in jazz that were an expression of the new cultural and political ferment that marked the rise of the mass struggle for Black rights. $24

Lenin's Final Fight
Speeches and Writings, 1922–23

V.I. LENIN

In the early 1920s Lenin waged a political battle in the Communist Party leadership in the USSR to maintain the course that had enabled workers and peasants to overthrow the tsarist empire, carry out the first socialist revolution, and begin building a world communist movement. The issues posed in this fight—from the leadership's class composition, to the worker-peasant alliance and battle against national oppression—remain central to world politics today. $21. Also in Spanish.

EXPAND *your Revolutionary Library*

Malcolm X
Talks to Young People

Four talks and an interview given to young people in Ghana, the United Kingdom, and the United States in the last months of Malcolm's life. This new edition contains the full 1964 talk to the Oxford Union in the UK, in print for the first time anywhere. The collection concludes with two memorial tributes by a young socialist leader to this great revolutionary. $15. Also in Spanish.

The History of the Russian Revolution

LEON TROTSKY

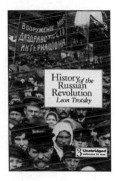

A classic account of the social, economic, and political dynamics of the first socialist revolution as told by one of its central leaders. "The history of a revolution is for us first of all a history of the forcible entrance of the masses into the realm of rulership over their own destiny," Trotsky writes. Unabridged edition, 3 vols. in one. $36

Puerto Rico:
Independence Is a Necessity

RAFAEL CANCEL MIRANDA

Rafael Cancel Miranda is one of five Puerto Rican Nationalists imprisoned by Washington for more than 25 years until 1979. In two interviews, he speaks out on the brutal reality of U.S. colonial domination, the campaign to free Puerto Rican political prisoners, the example of Cuba's socialist revolution, and the resurgence of the independence movement today. $5. Also in Spanish.

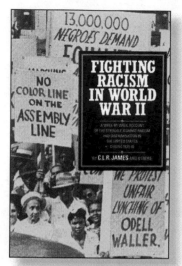

Fighting Racism in World War II
C.L.R. JAMES, EDGAR KEEMER,
GEORGE BREITMAN
A week-by-week account of the struggle
against lynch-mob terror and racist discrimination in U.S. war industries, the armed forces,
and society as a whole from 1939 to 1945, taken
from the pages of the socialist newsweekly, the
Militant. These struggles helped lay the basis
for the rise of the mass civil rights movement
in the subsequent two decades. $21.95

Workers of the World
and Oppressed Peoples, Unite!
*Proceedings and Documents of the Second Congress
of the Communist International, 1920*
The debate among delegates from 37 countries
takes up key questions of working-class strategy
and program—the fight for national liberation,
the revolutionary transformation of trade unions,
the worker-farmer alliance, participation in elections and parliament, and the structure and
tasks of Communist Parties. The reports, resolutions, and debates offer a vivid portrait of social
struggles in the era of the Bolshevik-led October
Revolution. 2 volumes, $36 each

Socialism on Trial
JAMES P. CANNON
The basic ideas of socialism, explained in
testimony during the trial of 18 leaders of the
Minneapolis Teamsters union and the Socialist
Workers Party framed up and imprisoned under
the notorious Smith "Gag" Act at the beginning
of World War II. $16. Also in Spanish.

Imperialism, the Highest Stage of Capitalism

V.I. LENIN

Imperialism increases not only the weight of debt bondage and parasitism in capitalist social relations, writes Lenin, but above all makes the competition of rival capitals—domestic and foreign—more violent and explosive. Amid capitalism's growing world disorder, this 1916 booklet remains a foundation stone of the communist movement's program and activity. $10

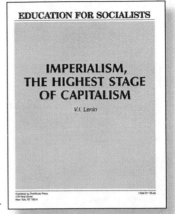

Pathfinder Was Born with the October Revolution

MARY-ALICE WATERS

From the writings of Marx, Engels, Lenin, and Trotsky, to the speeches of Malcolm X, Fidel Castro, and Che Guevara, to the words of James P. Cannon, Farrell Dobbs, and leaders of the communist movement in the U.S. today, Pathfinder books aim to "advance the understanding, confidence, and combativity of working people." $3. Also in Spanish and French.

The Jewish Question
A Marxist Interpretation

ABRAM LEON

Traces the historical rationalizations of anti-Semitism to the fact that, in the centuries preceding the domination of industrial capitalism, Jews emerged as a "people-class" of merchants, moneylenders, and traders. Leon explains why the propertied rulers incite renewed Jew-hatred in the epoch of capitalism's decline. $20

New International

A MAGAZINE OF MARXIST POLITICS AND THEORY

NEW INTERNATIONAL NO. 12

CAPITALISM'S LONG HOT WINTER HAS BEGUN

Jack Barnes

and "Their Transformation and Ours," Resolution of the Socialist Workers Party

Today's sharpening interimperialist conflicts are fueled both by the opening stages of what will be decades of economic, financial, and social convulsions and class battles, as well as by the most far-reaching shift in Washington's military policy and organization since the U.S. buildup toward World War II. Class-struggle-minded working people must face this historic turning point for imperialism, and draw satisfaction from being "in their face" as we chart a revolutionary course to confront it. $16

NEW INTERNATIONAL NO. 13

OUR POLITICS START WITH THE WORLD

Jack Barnes

The huge inequalities between imperialist and semicolonial countries, and among classes within almost every country, are produced, reproduced, and accentuated by the workings of capitalism. For vanguard workers to build parties able to lead a successful revolutionary struggle for power in our own countries, says Jack Barnes, our activity must be guided by a strategy to close this gap.

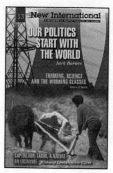

Also includes: "Farming, Science, and the Working Classes" *by Steve Clark* and "Capitalism, Labor, and Nature: An Exchange" *by Richard Levins, Steve Clark.* $14

NEW INTERNATIONAL NO. 9

THE RISE AND FALL OF THE NICARAGUAN REVOLUTION

Based on ten years of socialist journalism from inside Nicaragua, this issue recounts the achievements and worldwide impact of the 1979 Nicaraguan Revolution. It traces the political retreat of the Sandinista National Liberation Front leadership that led to the downfall of the workers and farmers government in the closing years of the 1980s. Documents of the Socialist Workers Party. $16

NEW INTERNATIONAL NO. 8

CHE GUEVARA, CUBA, AND THE ROAD TO SOCIALISM

Articles by Ernesto Che Guevara, Carlos Rafael Rodríguez, Carlos Tablada, Mary-Alice Waters, Steve Clark, Jack Barnes

Exchanges from the opening years of the Cuban Revolution and today on the political perspectives defended by Guevara as he helped lead working people to advance the transformation of economic and social relations in Cuba. $10

NEW INTERNATIONAL NO. 10

DEFENDING CUBA, DEFENDING CUBA'S SOCIALIST REVOLUTION

Mary-Alice Waters

In face of the greatest economic difficulties in the history of the revolution in the 1990s, Cuba's workers and farmers defended their political power, their independence and sovereignty, and the historic course they set out on at the opening of the 1960s. *Also includes* "Imperialism's March toward Fascism and War" *by Jack Barnes.* $16

NEW INTERNATIONAL NO. 11

U.S. IMPERIALISM HAS LOST THE COLD WAR

Jack Barnes

Contrary to imperialist expectations at the opening of the 1990s in the wake of the collapse of regimes across Eastern Europe and the USSR claiming to be communist, the workers and farmers there have not been crushed. Nor have capitalist social relations been stabilized. The toilers remain an intractable obstacle to imperialism's advance, one the exploiters will have to confront in class battles and war. $16

PATHFINDER AROUND THE WORLD

Visit our website for a complete list of titles and to place orders

www.pathfinderpress.com

PATHFINDER DISTRIBUTORS

UNITED STATES
(and Caribbean, Latin America, and East Asia)

Pathfinder Books, 306 W. 37th St., 10th Floor,
New York, NY 10018

CANADA

Pathfinder Books, 2238 Dundas St. West, Suite 201,
Toronto, ON M6R 3A9

UNITED KINGDOM
(and Europe, Africa, Middle East, and South Asia)

Pathfinder Books, First Floor, 120 Bethnal Green Road
(entrance in Brick Lane), London E2 6DG

SWEDEN

Pathfinder böcker, Bildhuggarvägen 17, S-121 44 Johanneshov

ICELAND

Pathfinder, Skolavordustig 6B, Reykjavík
Postal address: P. Box 0233, IS 121 Reykjavík

AUSTRALIA
(and Southeast Asia and the Pacific)

Pathfinder, Level 1, 3/281-287 Beamish St., Campsie, NSW 2194
Postal address: P.O. Box 164, Campsie, NSW 2194

NEW ZEALAND

Pathfinder, 7 Mason Ave. (upstairs), Otahuhu, Auckland
Postal address: P.O. Box 3025, Auckland 1140

Join the Pathfinder Readers Club
to get 15% discounts on all Pathfinder titles
and bigger discounts on special offers.
Sign up at www.pathfinderpress.com
or through the distributors above.